The Gen X Series

IMO NSO NCO IEO

International Mathematics Olympiad | National Science Olympiad | National Cyber Olympiad | International English Olympiad

OLYMPIAD SAMPLE PAPERS 1

Useful for Olympiads Conducted at School, National & International Levels

Compiled By
Editorial Board

Strictly According to the Latest Syllabus of Olympiad

V&S PUBLISHERS

Published by:

V&S PUBLISHERS

F-2/16, Ansari road, Daryaganj, New Delhi-110002
☎ 23240026, 23240027 • *Fax:* 011-23240028
Email: info@vspublishers.com • *Website:* www.vspublishers.com

Regional Office : Hyderabad
5-1-707/1, Brij Bhawan (Beside Central Bank of India Lane)
Bank Street, Koti, Hyderabad - 500 095
☎ 040-24737290
E-mail: vspublishershyd@gmail.com

Branch Office : Mumbai
Jaywant Industrial Estate, 1st Floor–108, Tardeo Road
Opposite Sobo Central Mall, Mumbai – 400 034
☎ 022-23510736
E-mail: vspublishersmum@gmail.com

ISBN 978-93-579422-6-3
New Edition

DISCLAIMER

Publisher's Note

The current decade has firmly established V&S Publishers as one of the Leading Publishers of General Trade Mass Appeal Books across popular genres along with Academic Books for School Children. Having been in publishing trade for over 40 years, we understand the need of the hour when it comes to Books. After successfully publishing around 600 titles in the last decade and establishing a pan India network of booksellers & distributors including ecommerce platforms – Amazon, Flipkart etc; we determined after a nation-wide market research in tier 1, 2 and 3 cities that preparatory materials for status-acquiring OLYMPIAD BOOKS is the need of the hour.

And in true spirit, the Olympiad books on Science, Maths, English and Cyber published for classes 1 to 10 was picked by students off the shelf in no time. It acquired the 'Bestseller' image. Encouraged by this huge acceptability of our Olympiad Series among parents, students and booksellers alike, we at V&S Publishers decided to take PREPARATION to the next level by bringing out another handholding masterpiece – Olympiad Sample Papers.

These Sample Papers are the virtual replicas of the actual exam papers.

Yes! These Sample Papers are the virtual replicas of the actual exam papers. Inclusion of two sets each for Science, Maths, English and Cyber subjects from classes 1 to 10 in respective books are believed to be adequate to prepare students mentally for 'live exam conditions.' Anything else would have been 'under-preparation' or over-preparation'

You will hardly be able to differentiate the Sample Papers from the Actual Exam Papers. All this has been made possible by the people who have been in their respective fields for years – coaching and guiding students to succeed in this vital exam.

P.S. While every care has been taken to ensure correctness of content, if you come across any error, howsoever minor, anywhere in the book, do not hesitate to discuss with your teachers while pointing that out to us in no uncertain terms.

We wish you All the Best!

Contents

INTERNATIONAL MATHEMATICS OLYMPIAD (IMO)

Mock Test Paper 1

Total Questions : 35 Time : 1 Hour

I M O
INTERNATIONAL MATHEMATICS OLYMPIAD

PATTERN AND MARKING SCHEME

Section	(1) Logical Reasoning	(2) Mathematical Reasoning	(3) Everyday Mathematics	(4) Achievers Section
No. of Questions	10	10	10	5
Marks per Questions	1	1	1	2

SYLLABUS

Section – 1 : Patterns, Odd One Out, Measuring Units, Geometrical Shapes, Spatial Understanding, Grouping, Analogy, Ranking Test, Problems based on Figures

Section – 2 : Numerals, Number Names, Number Sense (2 digit numbers), Addition, Subtraction, Lengths, Weights and Comparisons, Time, Money, Geometrical Shapes and Solids, Patterns.

Section – 3: Syllabus as per Section 2.

Section – 4: Higher Order Thinking Questions – Syllabus as per Section 2.

LOGICAL REASONING

1. Choose the item that does not belong to the group?

(A)  (B) 

(C) 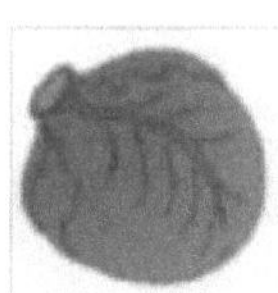 (D) 

2. Find the matching pair.

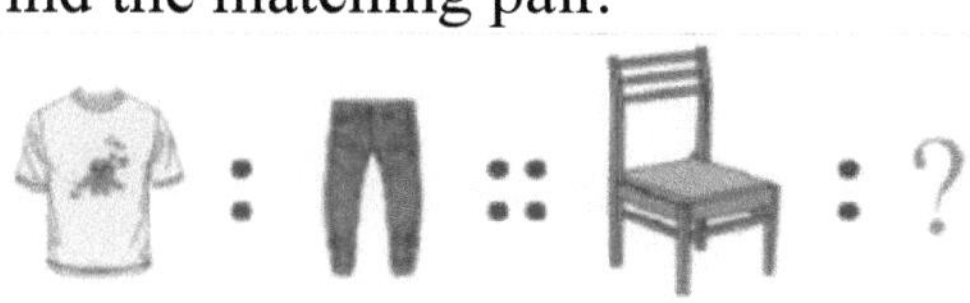

(A)  (B) 

(C)  (D) 

3. Look at the following table:

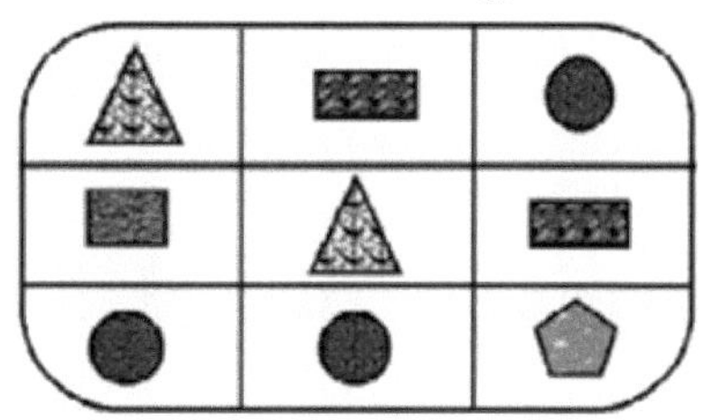

Which figure is in the centre of the table ?

(A) 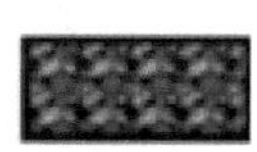 (B) 

(C)  (D) 

4. Which object is exactly the same as the one given?

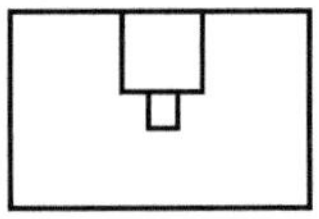

(A) 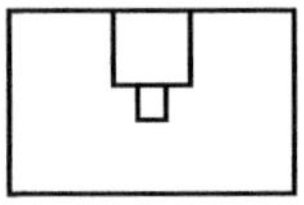 (B) 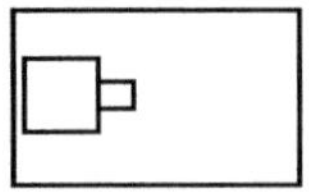

(C) 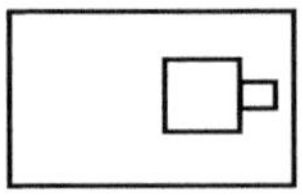 (D) 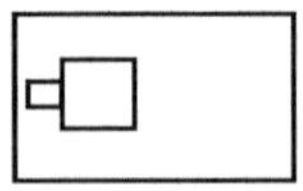

5. Identify the shape of the given figure

(A) Triangle (B) Rectangle
(C) Circle (D) Cuboid

6. Identify the object that belongs to the group.

(A)  (B) 

(C)  (D) 

7. Which leaf is the longest?

(A) 

(B) 

(C) 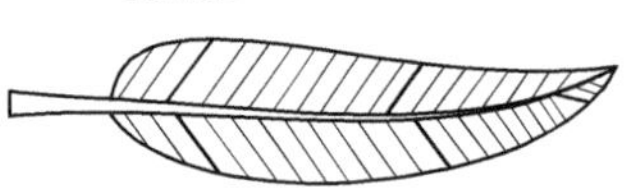

(D) 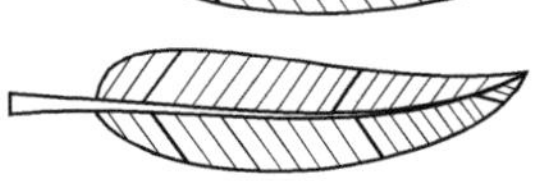

8. Complete the picture from the options given below.

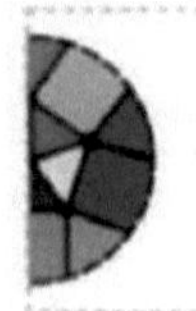

(A) 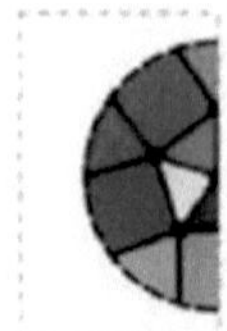 (B) 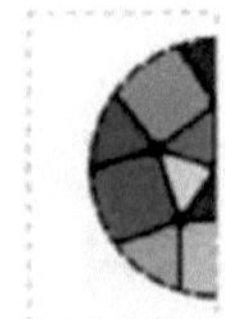

(C) 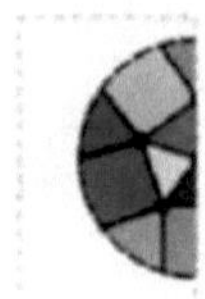 (D) 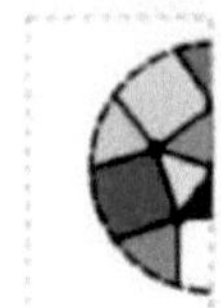

9. Which joker is third from the left end?

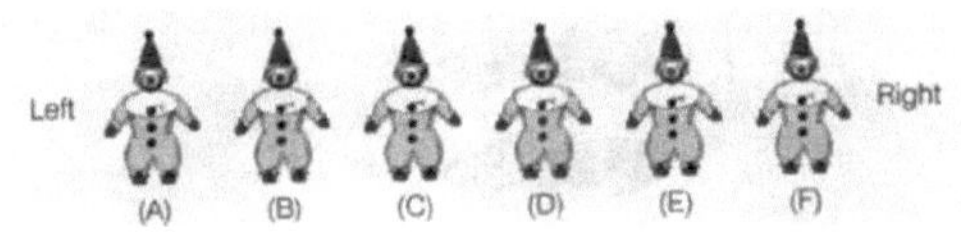

(A) D (B) F
(C) E (D) C

10. Which one comes next?

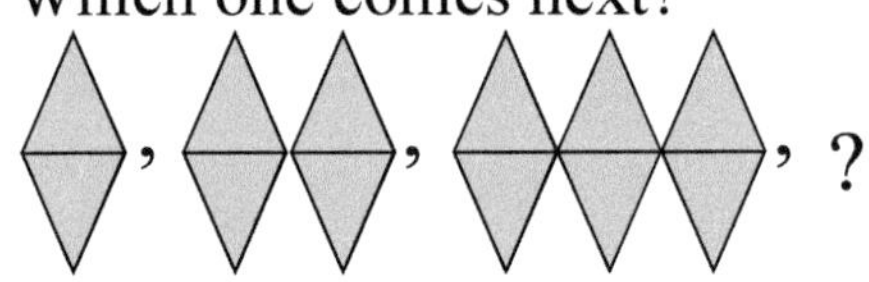

(A) 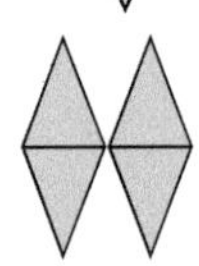

(B) 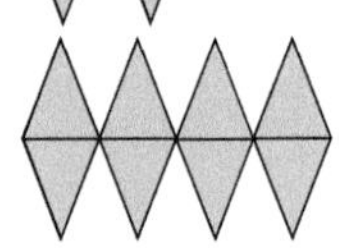

(C) 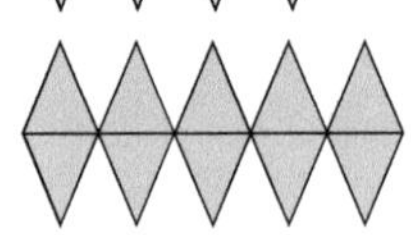

(D) 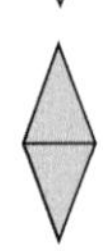

MATHEMATICAL REASONING

11. What is 6 more than 8?
(A) 14 (B) 0
(C) 68 (D) 12

12. Choose the largest 4- digit number.
(A) 0019 (B) 0999
(C) 9999 (D) 1000

13. Raj is playing with some numbered cards. Find the sum of all numbers given on cards.

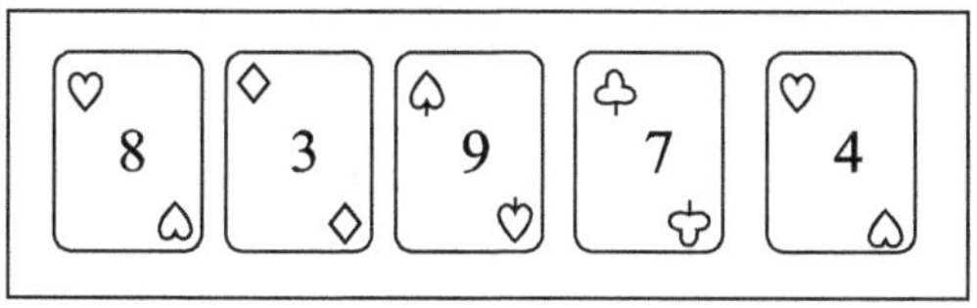

(A) 41 (B) 31
(C) 28 (D) 30

14. How is 20 less than 69 written?
(A) 69 – 40 = 29
(B) 69 – 2 = 67
(C) 69 – 20 = 49
(D) 69 – 12 = 57

15. When the hour hand is at 3 and the minute hand is at 12. Which time is shown by the clock?
(A) 3 O' clock (B) 5 O' clock
(C) 2 O' clock (D) 4 O' clock

16. Mayank bought some eggs for breakfast. In which shape is it?

(A) 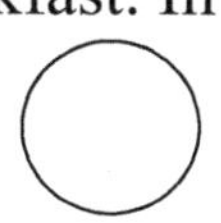 (B) 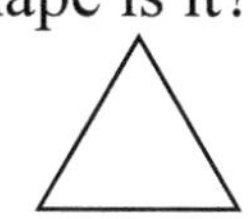

(C) 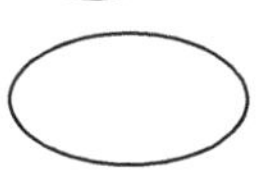 (D) 

17. Look at the picture graph and find the number of books sold on Wednesday.

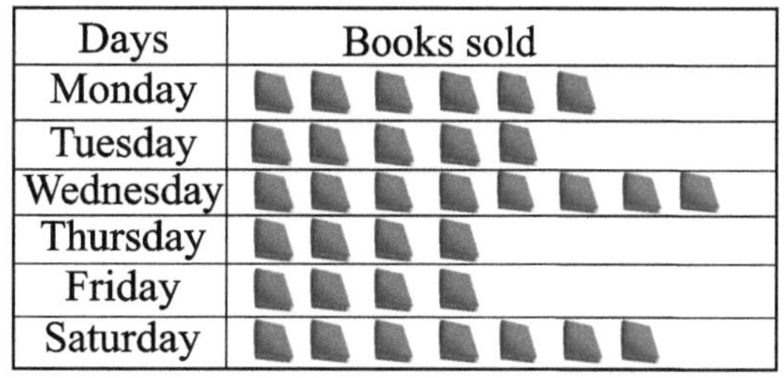

(A) 10 (B) 8
(C) 6 (D) 7

18. Sheena wants to buy the two toys shown here.

How much she has to pay altogether?
(A) ₹ 180 (B) ₹ 140
(C) ₹ 160 (D) ₹ 200

19. The amount of space inside an object is called ___________.
(A) Measuring Jar
(B) Capacity
(C) Weight
(D) Length

20. Find the ordinal number 20?
(A) Thirty (B) Fourteen
(C) Twenty (D) Eighteen

21. In which place is the  in the box given?

(A) Third (B) First
(C) Fourth (D) Third

22. Esha wants to arrange a surprise birthday party for her brother. She goes to market to buy two sets of candles given below.

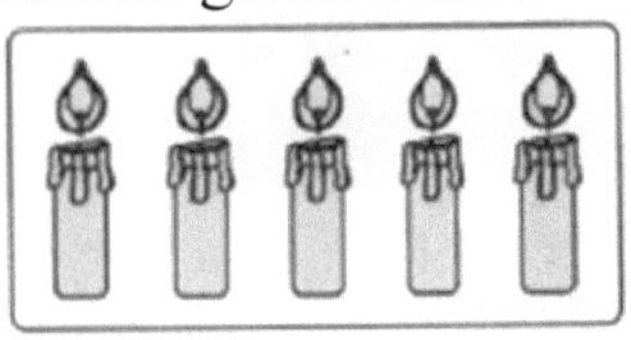

Find the number of candles she buys?
(A) 10 (B) 9
(C) 8 (D) 20

23. Aryan was given a task by his mother to choose the correct clock that shows the time as 11:35.

(A)  (B) 

(C)  (D) 

24. Look at the picture graph which shows the number of buses manufactured during a year.

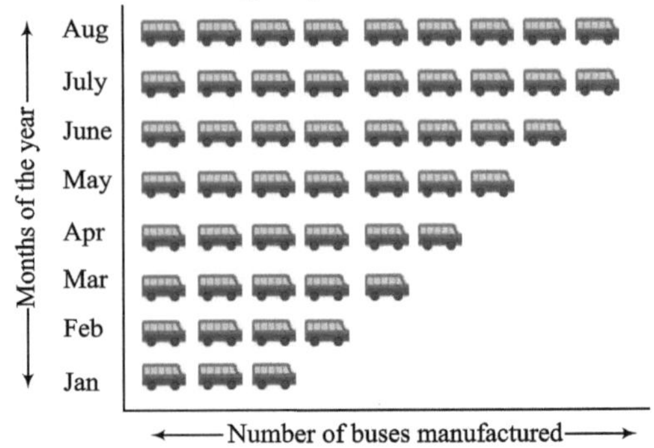

Find the number of buses manufactured in the month of July and August altogether.
(A) 9 (B) 7
(C) 5 (D) 18

25. Sakshi is moving upstairs by counting the numbers marked on stairs. While moving she found that one number is missing in the ascending order. Identify the number.

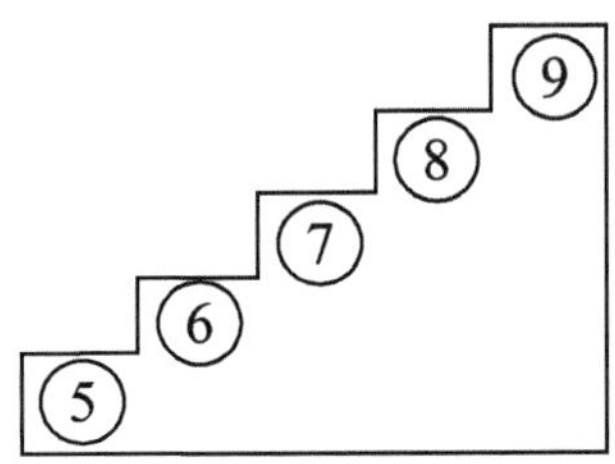

(A) 12 (B) 10
(C) 15 (D) 9

26. There is a drawing competition on Independence Day in Ishan's school. He has to draw a flag for the competition.

Choose the correct sequence from the following options in drawing a flag as per the pictures shown below.

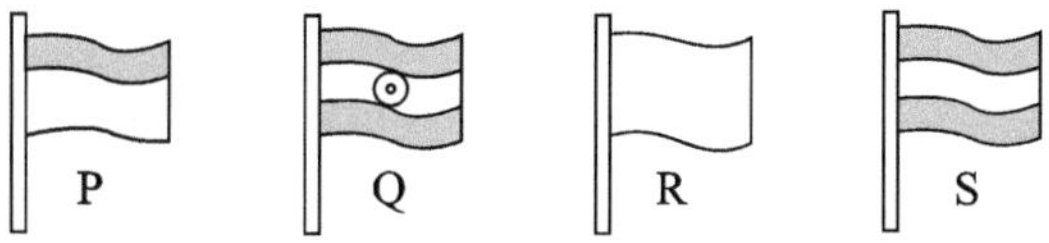

(A) P, Q, R, S (B) P, S, Q, R
(C) R, S, Q, P (D) R, P, S, Q

27. Diya gave ₹ 40 to buy this toy. How much will she get back?

(A) ₹ 25 (B) ₹ 10
(C) ₹ 15 (D) ₹ 20

28. Mary wants to measure a pencil given below by using paper clips. How many clips would be equal to the length of the pencil.

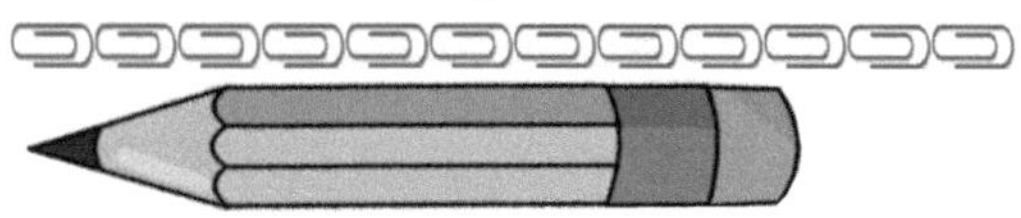

(A) 12 (B) 9
(C) 8 (D) 10

29. The picture given below shows a box that contains some keys. Some of them cannot be used. Find the number of keys that are in good condition.

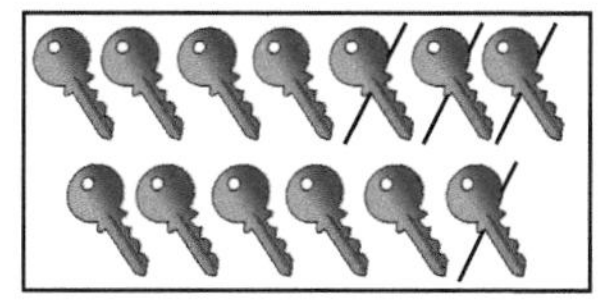

(A) 9 (B) 13
(C) 5 (D) 17

30. Rohan is playing with a dice. When he rolled a dice once, he got a number which is 1 less than 5. Identify the number.

(A) 3 (B) 6
(C) 4 (D) 2

ACHIEVERS SECTION

31. Identify the measuring jar which has the least capacity.

(A) 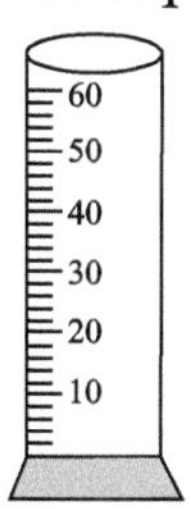

(B) 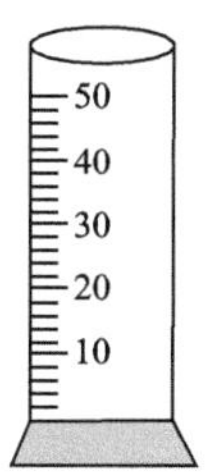

(C) 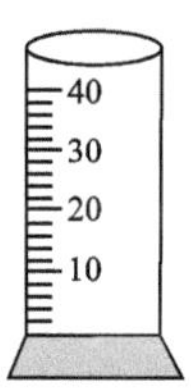

(D) 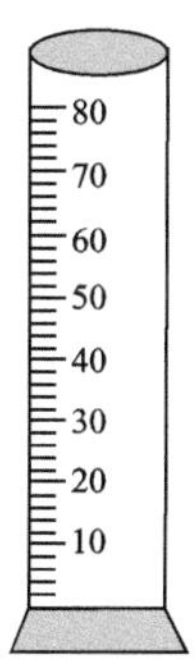

32. An organization is open for 5 days in a week. How many days are working in the month of June?

June	
Day	**Number**
Sunday	4
Monday	4
Tuesday	4
Wednesday	5
Thursday	4
Friday	5
Saturday	4

(A) 22 days (B) 25 days
(C) 16 days (D) 22 days

33. Find the number of circles in the given figure

(A) 10 (B) 18

(C) 12 (D) 15

34. Rashmi wants to buy the given parrot and she has ₹ 40. How much more money does she need?

₹ 55

(A) ₹ 10 (B) ₹ 30

(C) ₹ 15 (D) ₹ 30

35. Which of the following clocks show 9 o' Clock ?

(A)  (B) 

(C)  (D) 

Mock Test Paper

2

Total Questions : 35 | Time : 1 Hour

I M O

INTERNATIONAL MATHEMATICS OLYMPIAD

PATTERN AND MARKING SCHEME				
Section	**(1) Logical Reasoning**	**(2) Mathematical Reasoning**	**(3) Everyday Mathematics**	**(4) Achievers Section**
No. of Questions	10	10	10	5
Marks per Questions	1	1	1	2

SYLLABUS

Section – 1 : Patterns, Odd One Out, Measuring Units, Geometrical Shapes, Spatial Understanding, Grouping, Analogy, Ranking Test, Problems based on Figures

Section – 2 : Numerals, Number names, Number Sense (2 digit numbers), Addition, Subtraction, Lengths, Weights and Comparisons, Time, Money, Geometrical Shapes and Solids, Patterns.

Section – 3: Syllabus as per Section–2.

Section – 4: Higher Order Thinking Questions – Syllabus as per Section–2.

LOGICAL REASONING

1. Find the matching pair.

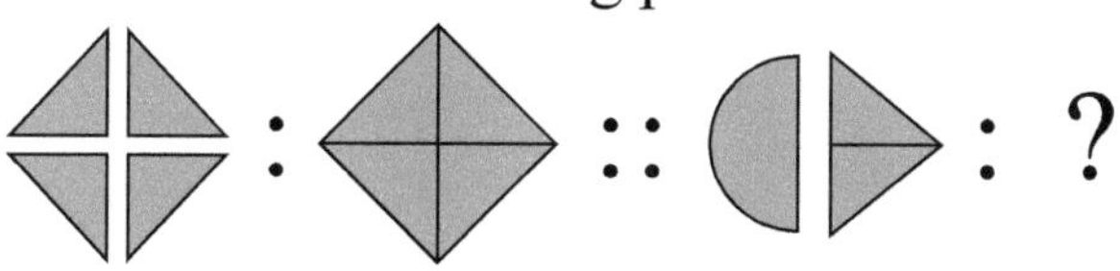

(A) 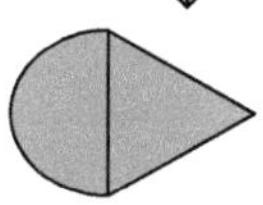 (B) 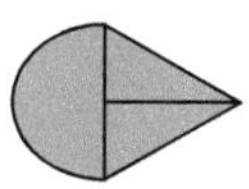

(C) 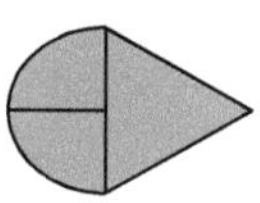 (D) 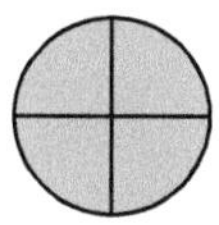

2. Number of fishes inside the net is ___________.

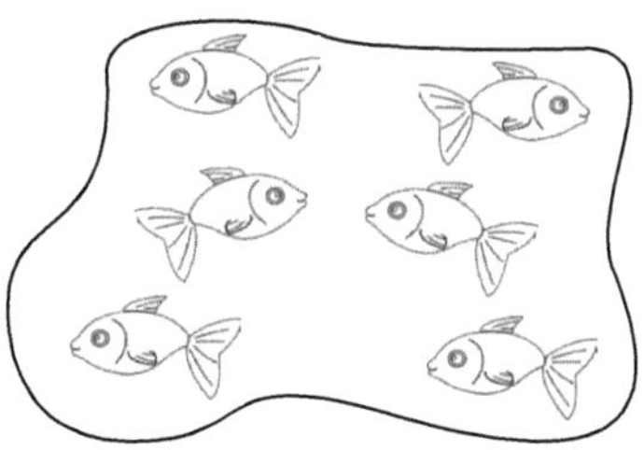

(A) 4 (B) 6

(C) 8 (D) 5

3. Find the odd one out.

(A)  (B) 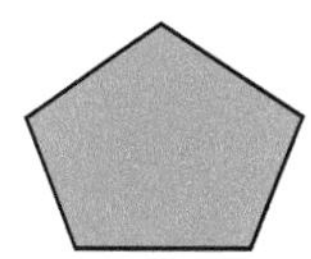

(C) 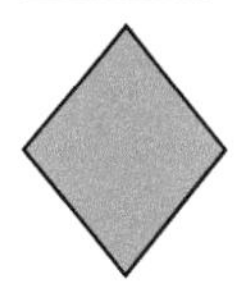 (D) 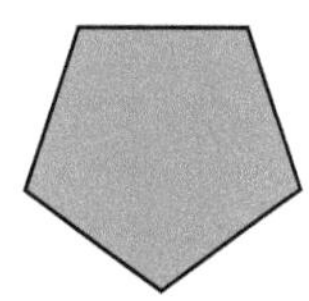

4. Which pencil is the longest ?

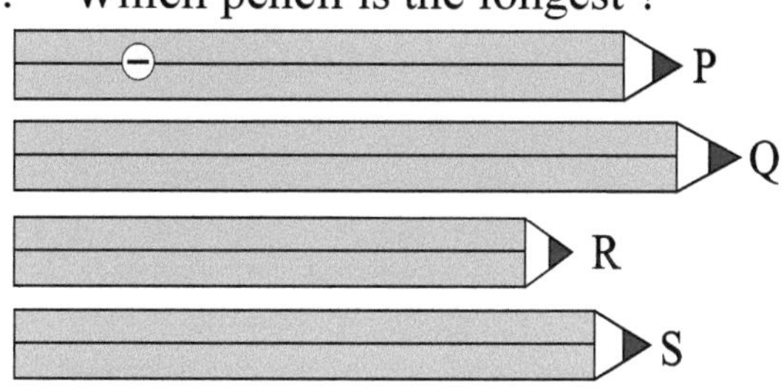

(A) Q (B) P

(C) R (D) S

5. Identify the cone from the given options.

(A) 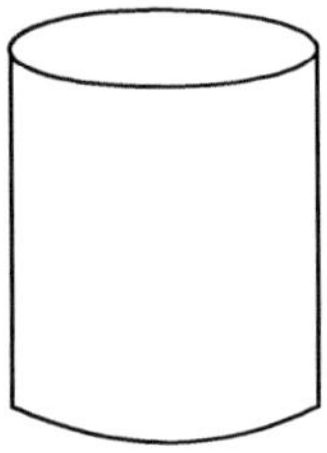

(B) 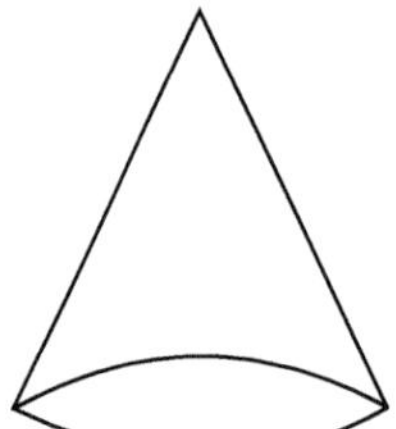

(C) 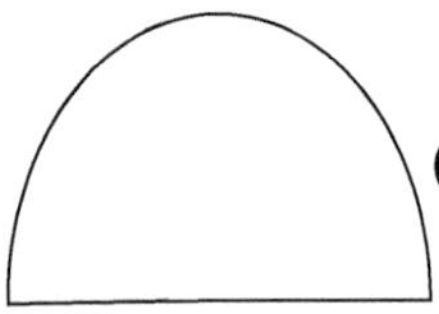

(D) 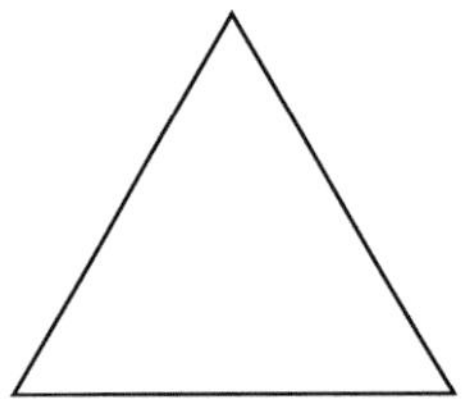

6. Choose the other half of the picture given below.

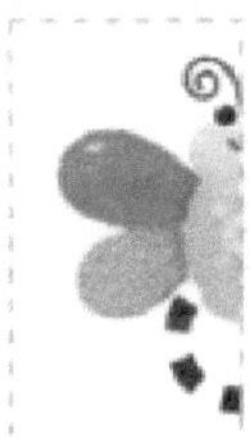

(A) 

(B) 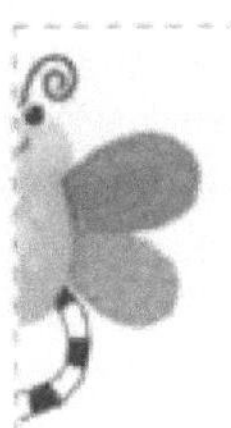

(C) 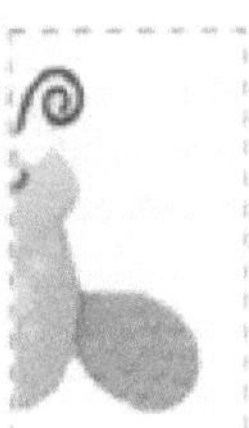

(D) 

7. Identify the missing pattern in the sequence below?

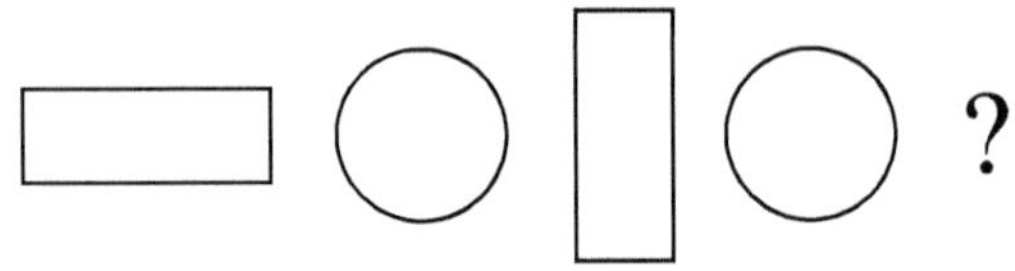

(A) 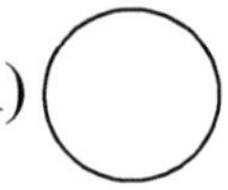

(B) 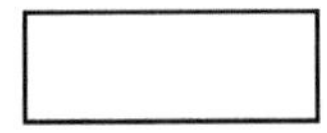

(C) 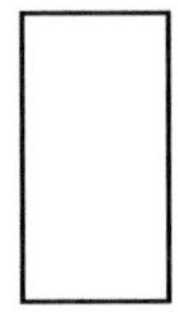

(D) 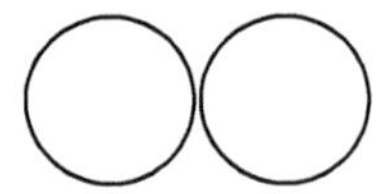

8. The shape of a notebook is _______.

(A) Rectangle (B) Cylinder

(C) Square (D) None of these

9. Identify the teddy which is at the fourth position from the last.

(A) G (B) C

(C) A (D) E

10. Identify the object that belongs to the given group.

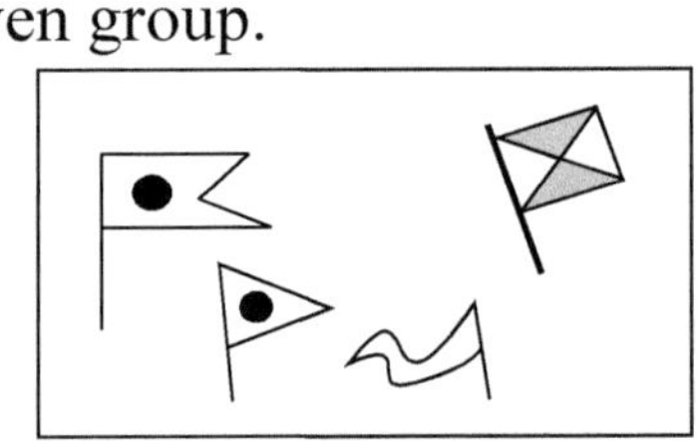

(A) 

(B) 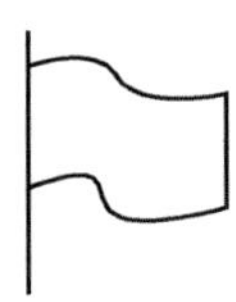

(C) 

(D) 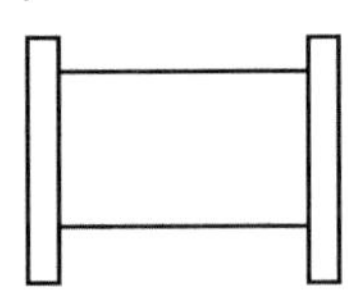

11. What is the short form of 'eight' ?
(A) 3rd (B) 8th
(C) 9th (D) 2nd

12. Anjali had 24 chocolates. She gave 5 to her sister. How many chocolates are left with her?
(A) 15 (B) 16
(C) 19 (D) 17

13. Identify the square which is smallest?

(A)  (B) 

(C)  (D) 

14. Ria wakes up early in the morning to go to school every day. Which clock shows the most ideal time?

(A)  (B) 

(C)  (D) 

15. Karan has ₹ 100 with him. He gets back ₹ 55 after buying a particular toy. Which of the following toy can he buy?

(A) 
₹ 50

(B) 
₹ 45

(C) 
₹ 60

(D) 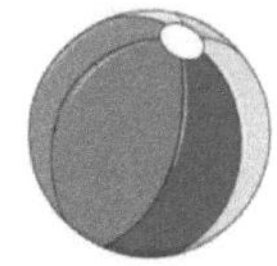
₹ 20

16. Look at the picture graph given below:

Count the number of pineapple.
(A) 8 (B) 6
(C) 5 (D) 4

17. Ashima puts some bangles on the table. In which shape are they?
(A) Cone (B) Circle
(C) Square (D) Cylinder

18. Find the sum represented by abacus.

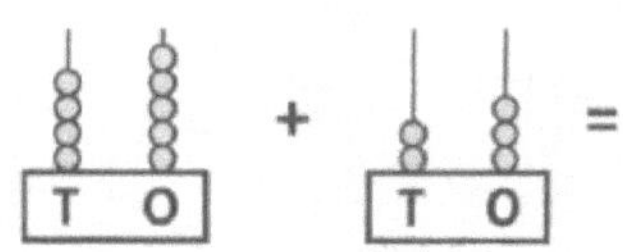

(A) 86 (B) 52
(C) 68 (D) 48

19. Which number is 4 less than 9 tens 3 ones?
(A) 87 (B) 98
(C) 89 (D) 97

20. What is the number name of smallest two-digit number?
(A) Thirteen (B) Eleven
(C) Ten (D) Zero

21. Which of the following is 1 more than 5?

(A) 

(B) 

(C) 

(D) 

22. Reena has a bowl that contains 47 *ladoos*. She puts 25 *ladoos* into it from another container. How many *ladoos* are there in the bowl altogether?

(A) 67 (B) 68
(C) 72 (D) 66

23. Harry puts his blocks in a box given below. What is the name of the shape of given box?

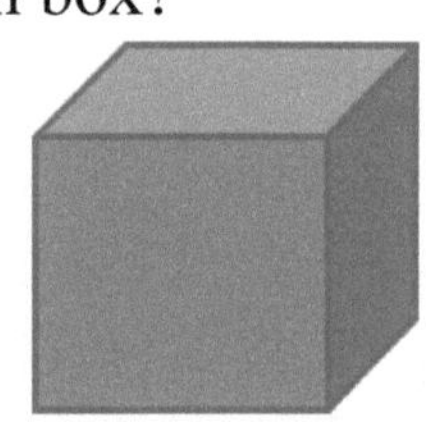

(A) Square (B) Rectangle
(C) Cuboid (D) Cube

24. Leena wants to buy an ice-cream given below. How much money she has to take out from her piggy bank to buy the ice-cream?

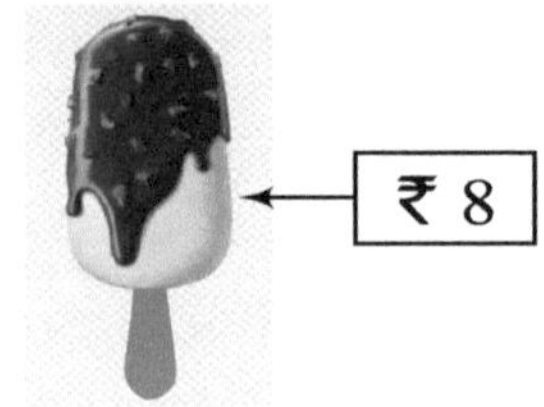

(A) ₹ 8 (B) ₹ 16
(C) ₹ 4 (D) ₹ 6

25. Meera wants to put given coffee mugs in a shelf according to ascending order of numbers marked on them. How can she arrange them in a shelf?

(A) 12, 32, 35, 38, 40
(B) 32, 12, 40, 38, 35
(C) 40, 35, 12, 38, 32
(D) 38, 40, 35, 12, 32

26. Look at the picture graph which shows the number of shells collected by four friends.

Anu	
Balu	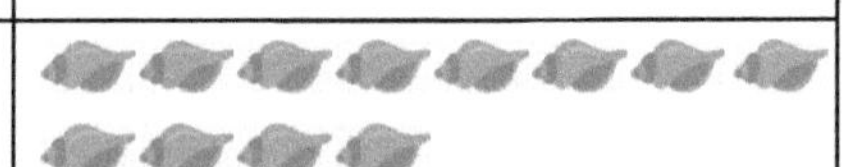
Raj	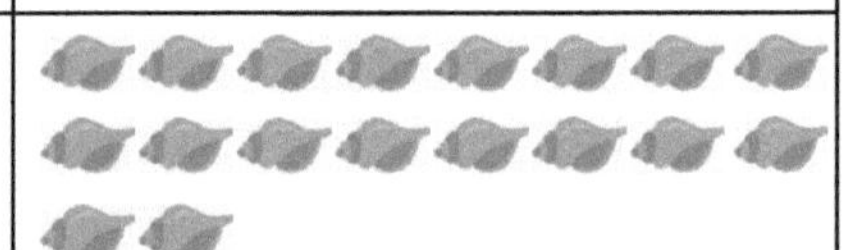
Salma	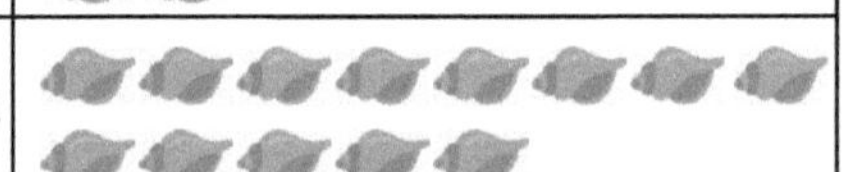

How many shells did Balu collect?

(A) 10 (B) 12
(C) 15 (D) 18

27. Saksham draws a clock for his assignment as given in the figure below.

What time does he wants to show?

(A) 10 : 45 (B) 9 : 50
(C) 9 : 45 (D) 10 : 40

28. Jiya is 168 cm tall and Latika is 12 cm taller than Jiya. How tall is Latika?
(A) 150 cm (B) 172 cm
(C) 180 cm (D) 190 cm

29. Arpit had some ice-cream cones given in the picture below. Out of which he gave 2 ice-creams to his brother. How many are left with him?

(A) 2 (B) 1
(C) 3 (D) 4

30. Riya is looking at some objects placed in the given set. She wants to know the third object from the right?

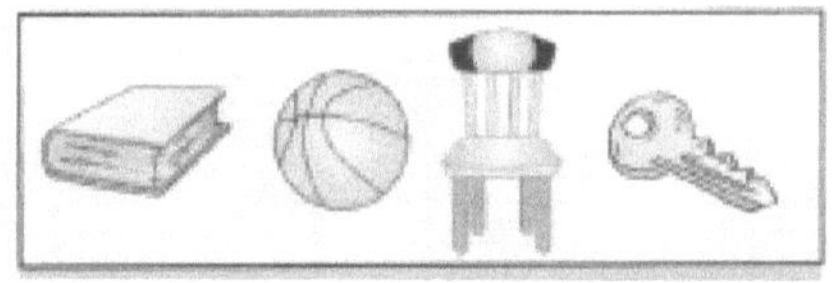

(A) Book (B) Key
(C) Chair (D) Ball

ACHIEVERS SECTION

31. Which of the following is the heaviest?

(A)  (B) 

(C)  (D) 

32. Which month has more than 30 days?
(A) April (B) June
(C) November (D) December

33. Count the number of balls in the given figure

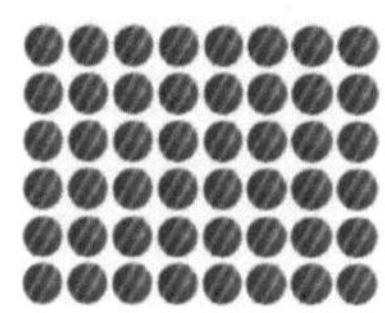

(A) 22 balls
(B) 48 balls
(C) 36 balls
(D) None of these

34. Which of the following looks like a sphere ?

(A)  (B) 

(C)  (D) 

35. Akhil wants to buy all the things shown here.

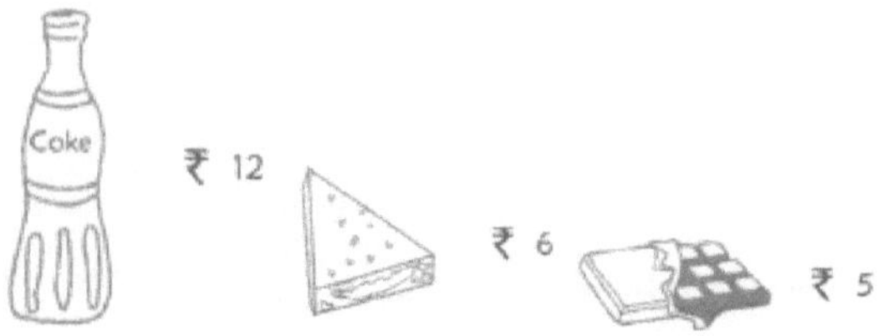

How much he has to pay?

(A) ₹ 23

(B) ₹ 32

(C) ₹ 50

(D) ₹ 20

NATIONAL SCIENCE OLYMPIAD (NSO)

Mock Test Paper **1**

Total Questions : 35 Time : 1 Hour

PATTERN AND MARKING SCHEME			
Section	**(1) Logical Reasoning**	**(2) Science**	**(3) Achievers Section**
No. of Questions	5	25	5
Marks per Questions	1	1	2

SYLLABUS

Section – 1 : Spatial Understanding, Grouping, Measuring Units, Analogy, Geometrical Shapes, Patterns, Odd One Out, Ranking Test

Section – 2 : Living and Non-living things, Plants, Animals, Human Beings and Their Needs, Good Habits and Safety Rules, Air and Water, Weather and The Sky.

Section – 3: Higher Order Thinking Questions – Syllabus as per Section – 2.

LOGICAL REASONING

1. Find the odd one out:

O 

P 

Q 

R 

(A) R (B) O
(C) P (D) Q

2. The shape of the coloured part is ________.

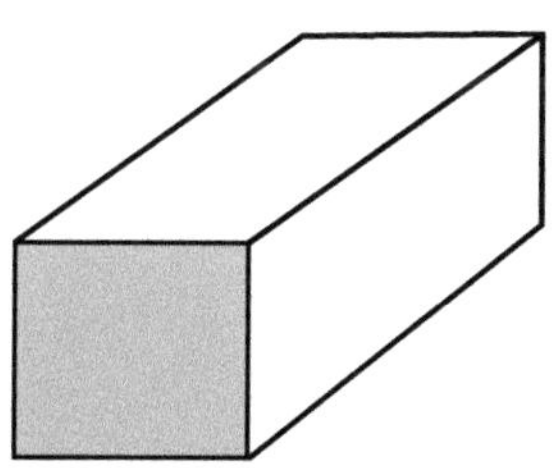

(A) Linear (B) Square
(C) Rectangle (D) Triangle

3. How many groups of 4 tigers can be formed from the given tigers?

(A) 8 (B) 4
(C) 2 (D) 6

4. Find the matching pair:

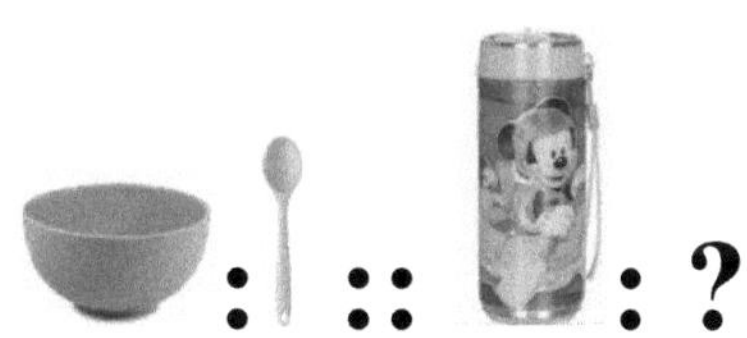

(A)  (B) 

(C)  (D) 

5. What will be the next?

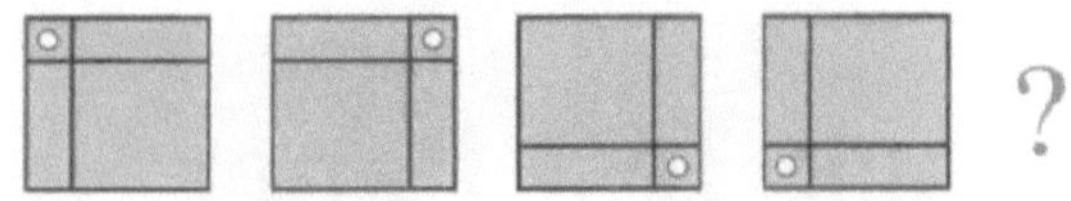

(A) 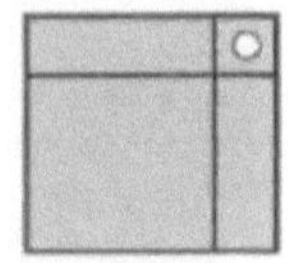 (B) 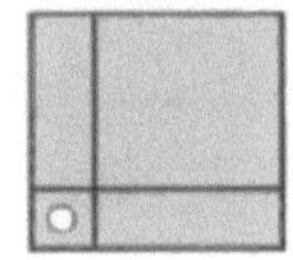

(C) 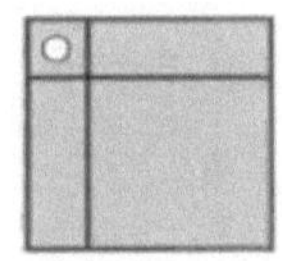 (D) 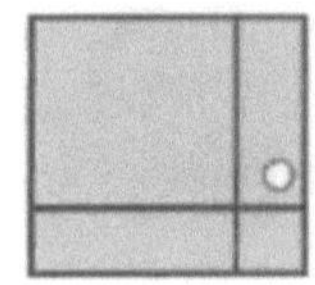

SCIENCE

6. Which is a living thing among the images below?

(A) 

(B) 

(C) 

(D) 

7. _____ is a type of food, which is received from the roots of the plants.

(A) 

(B) 

(C) 

(D) 

8. Which animal feeds upon only plants?
(A) Elephant (B) Lion
(C) Dog (D) Cat

9. _______ is the sensory organ which helps you to find your favourite cake.
(A) Nose
(B) Ear
(C) Both of these
(D) None of these

10. The last activity you should do before going to bed is _________.
(A) Watch your favorite cartoon
(B) Brush your teeth
(C) Eat lots of sweets
(D) All of these

11. Water is necessary for ________.
   (A) Washing the utensils
   (B) Cooking the food
   (C) Wiping the dirty surface
   (D) All of these

12. The first Indian who stepped on the moon was ________.
   (A) Sunita Williams
   (B) Rakesh Sharma
   (C) APJ Abdul Kalam
   (D) Kalpana Chawla

13. Which of the following statements is incorrect?
   (A) All living things occur naturally
   (B) Each and every man-made thing is non-living
   (C) All naturally occurring things are called as living things.
   (D) All non-living things are not made by human being

14. Vikrant introduced his father as a farmer and said that the crop he grows is used for extraction of oil. His father grows ________.
   (A) Wheat (B) Brinjal
   (C) Mustard (D) All of these

15. The animals which can live in both water and air are ________.
   (A) Frogs (B) Lion
   (C) Rabbit (D) All of these

16. In the chilly winter season, when someone touches you, you feel cold because of which sensory organ?
   (A) Tongue (B) Skin
   (C) Nose (D) Ear

17. We need food because ________.
   (A) It provides nutrition.
   (B) It keeps us healthy
   (C) Both (A) and (B)
   (D) None of these

18. How do you keep yourself safe?
   (A) By walking in the middle of the road.
   (B) By walking at the left side of the road.
   (C) By crossing the road when the traffic signal is green for vehicles
   (D) By going straight on the road without looking at left and right.

19. To become favourite of everybody, a kid should have the qualities as ________.
   (A) Discarding the wastes in the dust-bins only
   (B) Covering the mouth while yawning
   (C) Turning off taps after the use
   (D) All of these

20. Observe the given activity and mark the correct option. What does the image show?

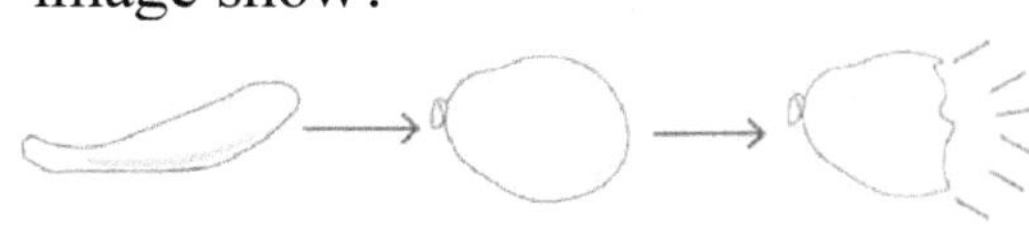

   (A) Air provides a shape to objects.
   (B) Air takes some space.
   (C) Air produces some amount of pressure.
   (D) All of these

21. In the winter seasons, what do you observe about sun rise and sun set?
   (A) Sun rises early, and sets delayed.
   (B) Sun rises late and sets early.
   (C) No effect on sunrising and sun-setting
   (D) None of these

22. If this symbol is given in the news paper in the weather report section, then what should you carry with you for your safety.

(A) Cakes and pastries
(B) Some medicines
(C) Raincoat or umbrella
(D) None of these.

23. Air is necessary for certain activities. Mark the set of activities, which requires air.
(A) Cooking food and blowing up a balloon.
(B) Cooking the food and washing the used utensils
(C) Flight of birds and dwelling on the land
(D) Blowing up a balloon and drying of the wet clothes

24. The suitable place for keeping the following things is __________.

(A) A first aid bo
(B) A safety match box
(C) A kitchen container
(D) A pencil box

25. Mark the correct pair.

(A)  For cycling

(B) 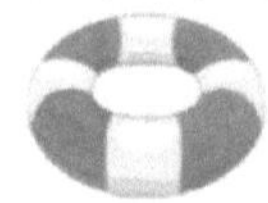 For swimming

(C) Both of these
(D) None of these

26. Anaya catches different infections very frequently. She should take more __________ in her diet.

(A) 

(B) 

(C) 

(D) 

27. The best time to eat your lunch is __________.
(A) 10 AM to 11 AM
(B) 12 Noon to 1 PM
(C) 2 PM to 3 PM
(D) Anytime

28. Read the following flow chart and mark the correct option.

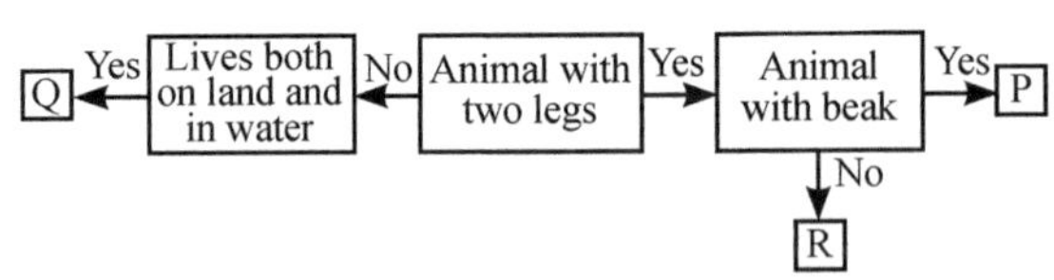

(A) P is Ostrich
(B) Q is crocodile

(C) R is kangaroo
(D) (A) and (C) are correct

29. What characteristics do these animals share in common?
Cow, monkey, elephant
(A) They live on the trees.
(B) They have a long trunk
(C) They feed upon the plants
(D) All of these

30. Nisha is a 2 years old girl. She is unaware of the types of plants. She goes in a garden with her elder brother. She gets attracted towards a beautiful flowe . When she tried to pluck that beautiful flowe , her finger got pricked and blood oozed out. The flower could be ___________.
(A) Marigold (B) Lily
(C) Sunflowe (D) Rose

ACHIEVERS SECTION

31. Observe the table and identify X, Y and Z

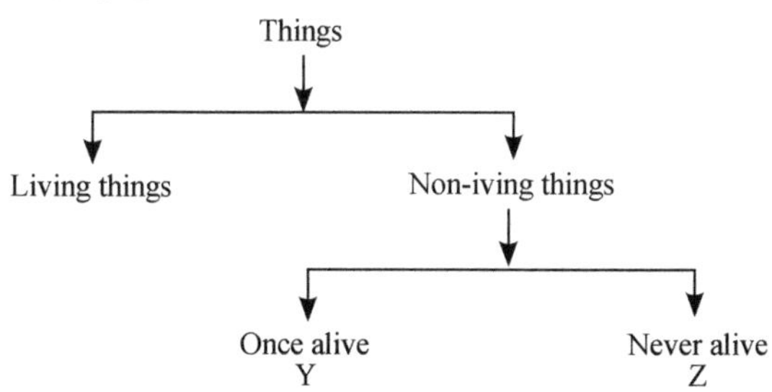

	X	Y	Z
(A)	Cow	Wooden table	Steel utensils
(B)	Rose	Steel Chair	Wooden table
(C)	Fruit	Ceramic cup	Steel utensils
(D)	Dol-phin	Cement	Wooden chair

32. Which of the following is best fitted in the place of X?

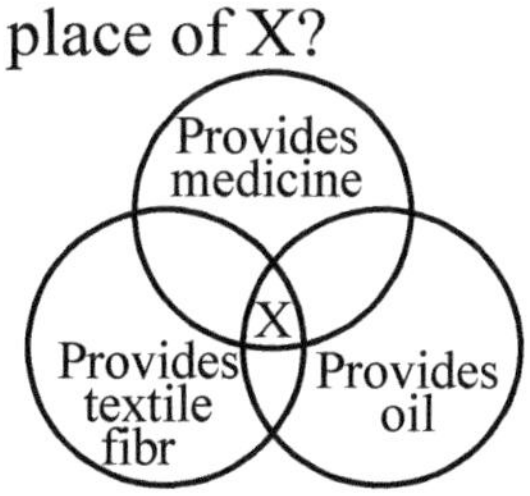

(A) Coconut
(B) Ground nut
(C) Mustard
(D) All of these

33. While moving on the road you see various sign boards. Every sign board indicates a specific rule. The given image indicates:

(A) Do not honk
(B) Do not cross the road
(C) Do not speak loudly on the road
(D) None of these

34. The given image indicates about a quality of the air. Identify the quality.

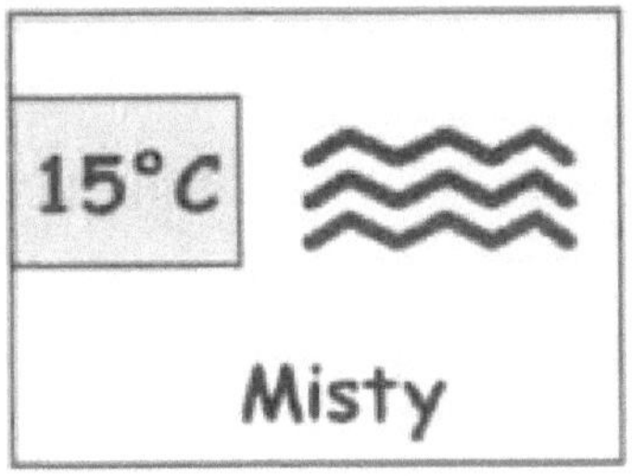

(A) Air has water vapours
(B) Air has water current
(C) Both of these
(D) None of these

35. Find the suitable set for P and Q.

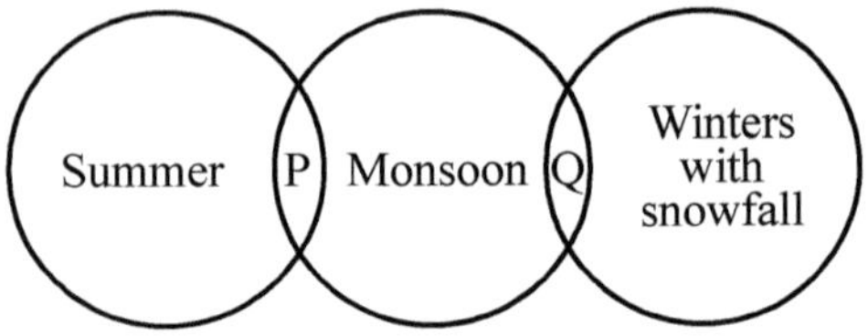

(A) P- raincoat Q- cap
(B) P- umbrella Q- Gloves
(C) Any of these
(D) None of these

Mock Test Paper 2

N S O

NATIONAL SCIENCE OLYMPIAD

Total Questions : 35 Time : 1 Hour

PATTERN AND MARKING SCHEME			
Section	**(1) Logical Reasoning**	**(2) Science**	**(3) Achievers Section**
No. of Questions	5	25	5
Marks per Questions	1	1	2

SYLLABUS

Section – 1 : Spatial Understanding, Grouping, Measuring Units, Analogy, Geometrical Shapes, Patterns, Odd One Out, Ranking Test

Section – 2 : Living and Non-living things, Plants, Animals, Human Beings and Their Needs, Good Habits and Safety Rules, Air and Water, Weather and The Sky.

Section – 3: Higher Order Thinking Questions – Syllabus as per Section – 2.

LOGICAL REASONING

1. Identify the soft toy which is placed on the third number from the right end?

(A) Q (B) R
(C) S (D) T

2. How many groups of flowers can be formed with 2 flowers in each group?

(A) 3 (B) 4
(C) 6 (D) 2

3. The difference between the number of circles and triangles is ________.

(A) 2 (B) 8
(C) 4 (D) 6

4. Month December comes just before _____ and just after ____.
(A) November, October
(B) October, January
(C) January, November
(D) November, January

5. What should come next?

(A) 75 (B) 65
(C) 80 (D) 10

SCIENCE

6. Choose the appropriate set of words to complete the paragraph given below.

   June is the month of _____ season, it is followed by July, a _____ season.

   (A) Summer, winter
   (B) Rainy, winter
   (C) Summer, windy
   (D) Summer, rainy

7. Rini is a class I student and lives in Lucknow. She made a set of festivals celebrated in India and the season of those festivals. But she made a mistake while pairing the season and festivals. Find the incorrect match.

	Festival	**Season**
(A)	Diwali	Cold days
(B)	Independence Day	Rainy days
(C)	Republic Day	Hot days
(D)	Raksha Bandhan	Rainy days

8. The shape of full moon looks like a _________.

   (A) Big white ball
   (B) Big white stone
   (C) Bunch of flower
   (D) None of these

9. We all live in a house. The house provides us protection from _______.

   (A) Sun heat
   (B) Rainfall
   (C) Cold and strong winds
   (D) All of these

10. Mark the incorrect statement.

   (A) Air exerts a pressure.
   (B) Air fills up space
   (C) We can see air.
   (D) We can feel air.

11. You play football. The shape of the football is round as seen in the image, because _________.

   (A) It is filled with wate .
   (B) It is filled with ai .
   (C) It is filled with both air and water.
   (D) None of these

12. This sign board indicates:

   (A) No parking zone
   (B) No walking zone

(C) No halt zone
(D) None of these

13. At school, during prayer, we should _________.
(A) Make a noise
(B) Stand in the queue
(C) Clap loudly
(D) All of these

14. To cross the road safely, we should _________.
(A) Use zebra crossing
(B) Run in the opposite direction of the cars
(C) Cross road by jumping
(D) None of these

15. Which of the following is a good habit?
(A) Trimming nails regularly
(B) Flushing the toilet after use
(C) Brushing your teeth two times daily.
(D) All of these.

16. Akash is a 4 years old smart kid. He made a set of seasons and clothes used in that season. Find the incorrect set.

	Season	Cloth
(A)	Winter	Woolen
(B)	Summer	Cotton
(C)	Rainy	Woolen
(D)	All are correct	

17. To make our teeth and bones strong, we should _________.
(A) Eat fast food
(B) Eat chocolate daily
(C) Drink a glass of milk
(D) Drink lots of soft drink.

18. Which sensory organ is in action in the given image?

(A) Eyes (B) Ears
(C) Skin (D) All of these

19. Which sensory organs will you use to play with video games?

(A) Ears and skin
(B) Eyes and ears
(C) Ears and nose
(D) Eyes and skin

20. Suppose, you are writing a poem on a paper. Which part of the body will you use for writing?
(A) Hand (B) Leg
(C) Ears (D) None of these

21. Mark the incorrect match of the animals and their sound.

	Animal	Sound
(A)	Lion	Roar
(B)	Cat	Meow
(C)	Dog	Bark
(D)	Frogs	Hum

22. Every living being needs a home for their safety. Ravika made some sets of the animals and their homes. Mark the correct set.

	Animal	Home
(A)	Spider	Web
(B)	Monkeys	Trees
(C)	Snakes	Burrows
(D)	All are correct	

23. Baby lions : Cubs :: Cow : ?
(A) Kitten (B) Calf
(C) Cub (D) Chick

24. The given image is a type of_______.

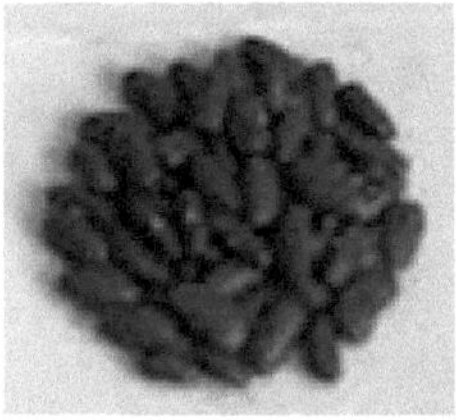

(A) Pulses (B) Lentils
(C) Grain (D) None of these

25. The yellow part of the plant is _____.

(A) Flower (B) Leave
(C) Stem (D) Fruit

26. Crops grow in the _________.
(A) Soil (B) Dust
(C) Water (D) Mountains

27. The image shows that _________.

(A) Human can smile
(B) Human can stand
(C) Human grows
(D) None of these

28. Bicycle is an example of _________.

(A) Living thing
(B) Non-living thing
(C) Both of these
(D) None of these

29. The living things and non-living things are different because of the characteristic(s) of ___________.
(A) Reproduction

(B) Growth
(C) Respiration
(D) All of these

30. Mark the incorrect statement.
(A) Non- living things grow in dark.
(B) Living things can grow.
(C) Natural things may be non- living.
(D) All of these

ACHIEVERS SECTION

31. When a burning candle is covered with a glass, after some time the candle blows off. What is the possible reason behind blowing off the candle?

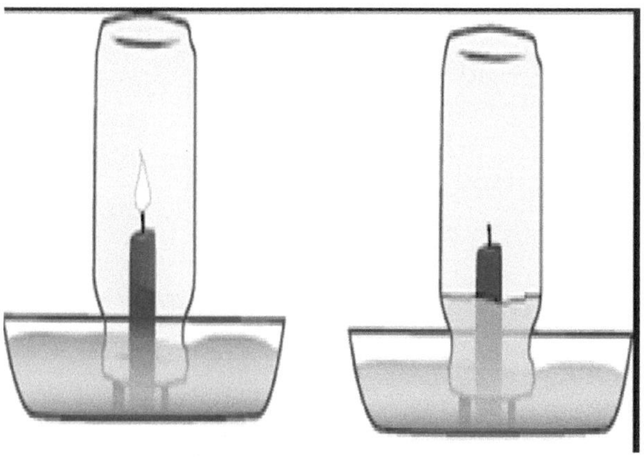

(A) Absence of space
(B) Absence of water
(C) Absence of air
(D) None of these

32. A gardener grows a tree of pomegranate. He takes care of the tree and waters it. One day his 10 years old daughter plucked some flowers of the tree. What will be the result of this action?
(A) The growth of the tree will decrease.
(B) All the leaves of the plant will shed down.
(C) The number of the fruits will reduce
(D) None of these

33. In the given image P, Q, and R are the parts of body. Identify the correct set of P, Q, and R.

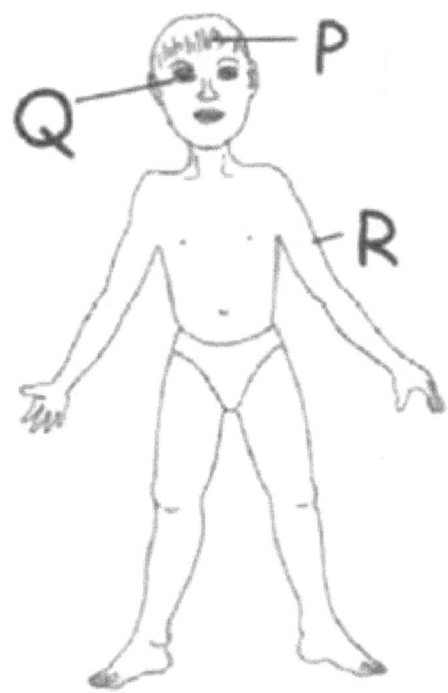

	P	Q	R
(A)	Hair	Nose	Hand
(B)	Head	Nose	Arm
(C)	Head	Eye	Arm
(D)	Hair	Nose	Hand

34. The given image shows that ______.

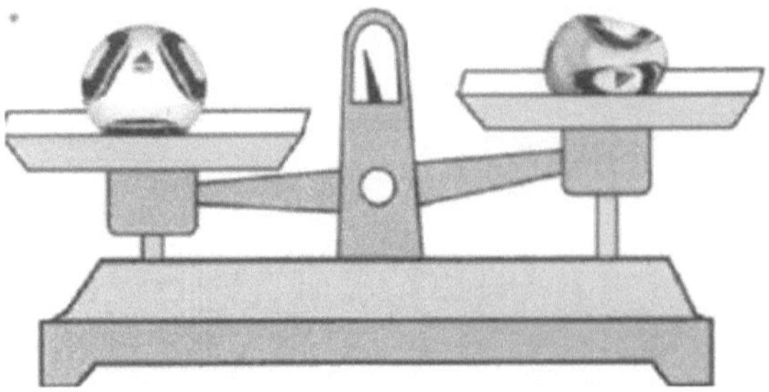

(A) Air has some weight
(B) Air has no weight
(C) The balance machine is working
(D) None of these

35. The given images show different shapes of moon. The name of the shapes of the moon are ________ respectively.

(A) Half-moon, Full moon, Crescent moon
(B) Crescent moon, half moon, full moon
(C) Crescent moon, full moon, half moon
(D) Any name can be given to any shape

NATIONAL CYBER OLYMPIAD (NCO)

Mock Test Paper 1

NCO

NATIONAL CYBER OLYMPIAD

Total Questions : 35 | Time : 1 Hour

PATTERN AND MARKING SCHEME			
Section	**(1) Logical Reasoning**	**(2) Computer and IT**	**(3) Achievers Section**
No. of Questions	5	25	5
Marks per Questions	1	1	2

SYLLABUS

Section – 1: Patterns, Completion of Figure Pattern, Measuring Units (Length, Weight, Time and Money), Geometrical Shapes, Odd One Out, Spatial Understanding, Grouping of Figures, Analogy, Ranking Test.

Section – 2: Introduction to Computers, Parts of Computer, Uses of Computer, Keys and Keyboard, Computer Mouse, Starting and Shutting down the Computer, Introduction to MS-Paint, Latest Developments in the field of I .

Section – 3: Higher Order Thinking Questions – Syllabus as per Section – 2.

LOGICAL REASONING

1. Select odd one out.

(A) 
(B) 
(C) 
(D) 

2. How many groups of 4 paper clips are there?

(A) 4 (B) 2
(C) 1 (D) 3

3. Which object is exactly the same as the one given below?

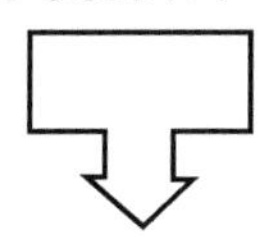

(A) 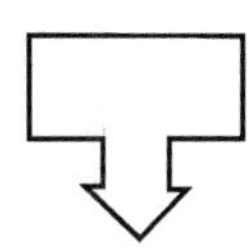
(B) 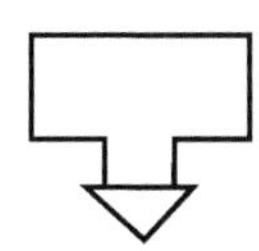
(C) 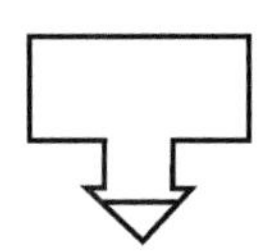
(D) 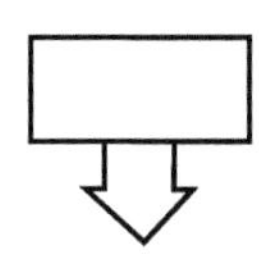

4. Find the missing number to complete the pattern.

(A) 14 (B) 21
(C) 22 (D) 8

5. Complete the analogy.

(A) 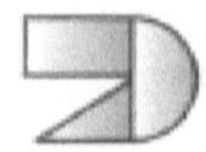 (B) 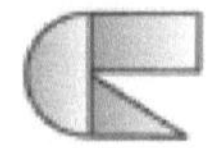

(C) 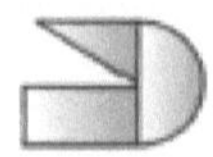 (D) 

COMPUTERS AND IT

6. Identify the following.

An electronic device that is used to play games.

(A)  (B) 

(C)  (D) 

7. __________ looks like a TV screen and shows whatever we type on the keyboard.
(A) Monitor (B) Mouse
(C) Printer (D) CPU

8. Identify the device that helps us to enter information into a computer with the help of buttons present on it.
(A) Monitor (B) Mouse
(C) Keyboard (D) Speakers

9. Identify the device that usually has two buttons and a small wheel.
(A) Keyboard (B) Monitor
(C) Mouse (D) Printers

10. A program that help us to draw and colour pictures is called _______.
(A) MS Paint (B) MS Word
(C) Power Point (D) None of these

11. Identify the gadget.

It has a touchscreen and allows you to use it with your fingers

It is portable and can easily fit in your pockets.
(A) Desktop (B) Smartphones
(C) Laptops (D) None of these

12. CPU stands for _________.
(A) Computer processing unit
(B) Control process unit
(C) Central Processing Unit
(D) None of these

13. Select the incorrect statement about the given part of the computer.

(A) It is an input device used to move a cursor around a screen.

(B) It is the brain of the computer.
(C) It is a hand operated device.
(D) It has a scroll wheel and two buttons.

14. Which of the following is an app?

(A)  (B) 

(C)  (D) None of these

15. Which of following is the wearable technology device?

(A)  (B) 

(C)  (D) None of these

16. Name the screen that appears when you turn on your computers that shows all the icons.
(A) Home page (B) Desktop
(C) Taskbar (D) Wallpaper

17. Which of the following tools in MS Paint is used to erase areas of your picture?
(A) Oval tool (B) Eraser tool
(C) Pencil tool (D) None of these

18. What is the use of the given tool?

(A) It is used to make rectangle shape.
(B) It is used to make straight lines.
(C) It is used for free-hand drawing.
(D) All of these

19. Select the incorrect match.

(A) 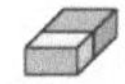 – It is used to erase your drawing.
(B)  – It is used for free hand drawing.
(C)  – It is used to fill the picture with colour.
(D)  – It is used to make rectangle shape.

20. A ________ is a man made machine which runs on ___________ and works very ______.
(A) computer, electricity, slow.
(B) computer, fuel, fast.
(C) computer, electricity, fast.
(D) television, electricity, fast.

21. Unscramble the options and select the one which is a part of a computer.
(A) BIRBON (B) OLVA
(C) MNOIRTO (D) BOOIGNT

22. Identify the key that helps to move the cursor to the right.

(A)  (B) 

(C) 

(D) 

23. Identify the following.
It contains all the drawing tools that are required to make a drawing.
(A) Ribbon Area
(B) Drawing area
(C) Color box
(D) None of these

24. Name the key which must be pressed to go to next line.
   (A) Delete key (B) Backspace key
   (C) Enter key (D) Shift key

25. Which of the following keys would you use to capitalizes each letter typed?

   (A) 

   (B) 

   (C) 

   (D) 

26. In banks, computers are used to ________.
   (A) maintain customer records and accounts.
   (B) play games.
   (C) diagnosing diseases.
   (D) None of these

27. Which of the following provides a surface for placing and moving a computer mouse?
   (A) Monitor (B) Mouse pad
   (C) Keyboard (D) Mouse pointer

28. The keys from A to Z are called ________.
   (A) Arrow keys (B) Special keys
   (C) Number keys (D) Alphabet keys

29. Which of the following part of computer is used for pointing items on screen?

   (A)  (B) 

   (C)  (D) 

30. Identify the odd one out device.

   (A)  (B) 

   (C)  (D) 

ACHIEVERS SECTION

31. Match the following.

Column I		Column II	
A.	Scrolling	(i)	Return Key
B.	Enter Key	(ii)	CPU
C.	Move the cursor down	(iii)	Moving the mouse wheel up or down
D.	Brain of a computer	(iv)	

   (A) A-(iii), B-(i), C-(iv), D-(ii)
   (B) A-(iii), B-(ii), C-(i), D-(iv)
   (C) A-(i), B-(iv), C-(iii), D-(ii)
   (D) A-(iv), B-(i), C-(ii), D-(iii)

32. Label the part of mouse from the given options.

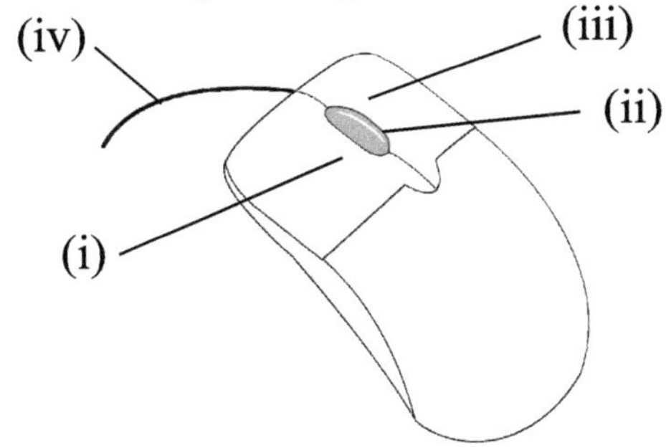

	(i)	(ii)	(iii)	(iv)
(A)	Tail	Right button	Wheel	Center button
(B)	Right button	Tail	Center button	Wheel
(C)	Left button	Scroll Wheel	Right Button	Tail
(D)	Wire	Scrolling	Right Button	Left Button

33. Identify the place where computers are used, with the help of statements given below.

Keeping records of books in the library.

Keeping student records.

(A) Sports (B) Hospitals
(C) Office (D) Schools

34. Which of the following statements is/are correct about the given device?

(A) It is used to print a copy of stored information on a sheet of paper.
(B) It keeps the computer working in case of power failure.
(C) It is used to type letters into the computer.
(D) It looks like a TV screen that displays information whatever we give as input.

35. Arrange the following steps in correct order to draw a rectangle shape in MS Paint.

i. Select the rectangle tool
ii. Open MS Paint.
iii. Click and drag the mouse once to draw a rectangle.
iv. Point the mouse on drawing area.

(A) i, iii, ii, iv (B) ii, i, iv, iii
(C) iv, i, iii, ii (D) ii, iii, i, iv

Mock Test Paper **2**

N C O
NATIONAL CYBER OLYMPIAD

Total Questions : 35 Time : 1 Hour

PATTERN AND MARKING SCHEME			
Section	**(1) Logical Reasoning**	**(2) Computer and IT**	**(3) Achievers Section**
No. of Questions	5	25	5
Marks per Questions	1	1	2

SYLLABUS

Section – 1: Patterns, Completion of Figure Pattern, Measuring Units (Length, Weight, Time and Money), Geometrical Shapes, Odd One Out, Spatial Understanding, Grouping of Figures, Analogy, Ranking test.

Section – 2: Introduction to Computers, Parts of Computer, Uses of Computer, Keys and Keyboard, Computer Mouse, Starting and Shutting down the Computer, Introduction to MS-Paint, Latest Developments in the field of I .

Section – 3: Higher Order Thinking Questions – Syllabus as per Section – 2.

LOGICAL REASONING

1. Complete the figure pattern

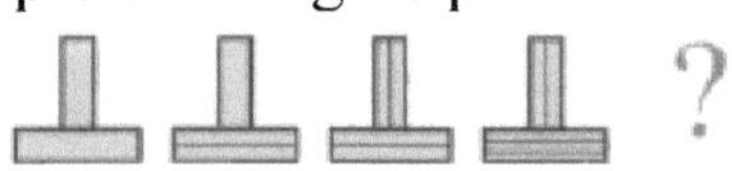

(A) 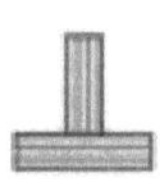 (B) 

(C) 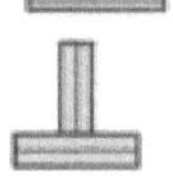 (D) 

2. Count the number of squares in the figure given belo .

(A) 6 (B) 10
(C) 8 (D) 10

3. Which of the following gift is 6th from the right end?

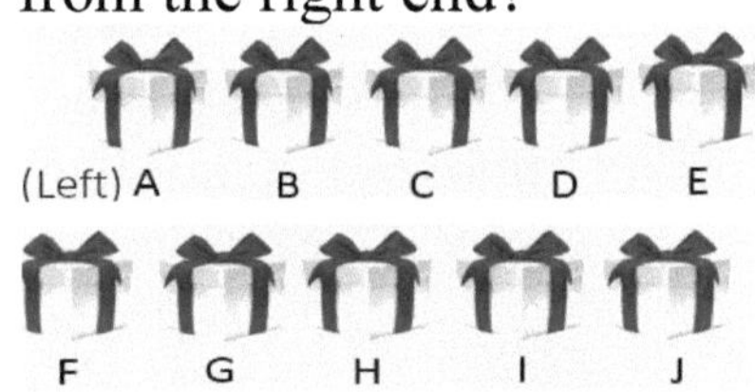

(A) F (B) D
(C) I (D) E

4. Which of the following costs the most?

(A)  (B) 

(C)  (D) 

5. Find the matching pair.

 :  ::  : ?

(A) 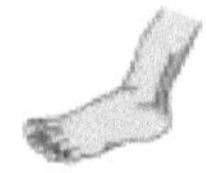
(B) 
(C) 
(D) 

COMPUTERS AND IT

6. Which of the following is called the brain of the computer?
(A) Monitor
(B) Keyboard
(C) CPU
(D) Printer

7. Which of the following part of computer is required to print the result of your work from the computer screen on a sheet of paper?
(A) Mouse
(B) Printer
(C) CPU
(D) Speakers

8. Select the incorrect match.

(A)  – Monitor

(B)  – Keyboard

(C)  – Speakers

(D)  – CPU

9. Which of the following key is used to move cursor left, right, up and down?
(A) Number key
(B) Alphabet key
(C) Caps lock key
(D) Arrow key

10. Pressing and releasing a button on mouse is called ________.
(A) Wiggling
(B) Clicking
(C) Scrolling
(D) None of these

11. ________ is the tool used to make oval shape.
(A) Rectangle
(B) Eraser
(C) Pencil
(D) Oval

12. Which of the following key would you use to insert space between the word?
(A) Delete key
(B) Spacebar key
(C) Shift key
(D) Backspace key

13. A mouse without a tail is called ________.
(A) Wired mouse
(B) Wireless mouse
(C) Keyboard
(D) None of these

14. Identify the following.
    An area of the paint window where we can draw shapes and pictures.
    (A) Paint Button
    (B) Drawing Area
    (C) Colour palette
    (D) None of these
15. The first step to shut down a computer is ________.
    (A) Switch off the UPS.
    (B) Click on Start Button.
    (C) Switch off the main power button.
    (D) Click on Shut Down.
16. Which of the following can be done by using computer in offices
    (A) Keeping employee records
    (B) Typing documents
    (C) Taking printouts
    (D) All of these
17. Select the incorrect match.
    (A) This key is used to insert space between words. – 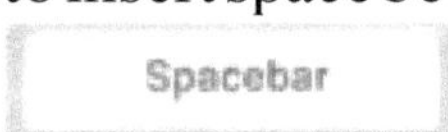

    (B) Capitalize letters – 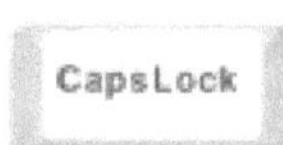

    (C) It is used to draw circles – 
    (D) Supply power to computer in case of power failure – 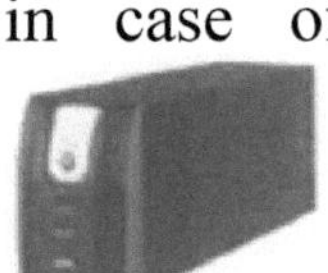
18. Which of the following tools in MS-paint helps you to draw the image given below?

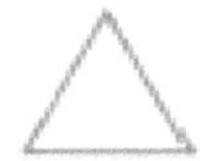

    (A)  (B) 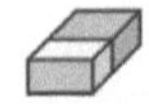
    (C)  (D) None of these
19. Which of the following action of a mouse opens an item on computer.
    (A) Single clicking
    (B) Booting
    (C) Double clicking
    (D) None of these
20. Which of the following device displays the output?
    (A)  (B) 
    (C)  (D) 
21. Select the correct statement about the given part of computer.

    (A) Used for listening to recorded sounds.
    (B) Used for pointing and selecting items on screen.
    (C) Used to take out the printout.
    (D) None of these

22. Unscramble the options and select the one which is a key on keyboard.

(A) MUOES (B) NABK
(C) NILE (D) RORWA

23. Identify the following.

They are the small pictures which you see on your desktop.

(A) Clips (B) Snaps
(C) Icons (D) None of these

24. Which of the following actions is being performed in the given image?

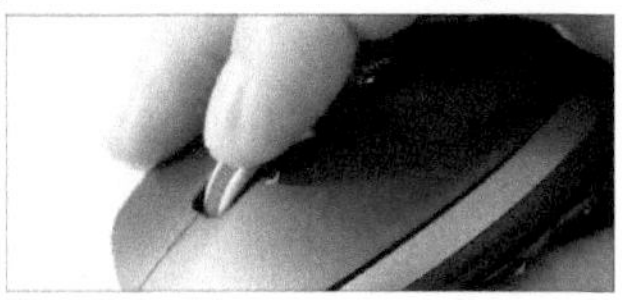

(A) Scrolling (B) Dragging
(C) Clicking (D) Double-click

25. The given image is of a wearable gadget known as _______.

(A) Smart watch (B) Stopwatch
(C) Time watch (D) None of these

26. Identify the following.

It is used to fill picture with colors

We can choose colors from color palette.

(A)  (B) 

(C) 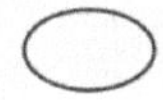 (D) 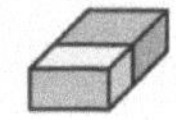

27. Which famous game is shown here?

(A) Angry Birds
(B) Candy Crush
(C) Clash Royale
(D) Pokémon

28. Name the part of the computer which is used to keep the computer on, when there is power failure?

(A) Mouse (B) CPU
(C) UPS (D) Keyboard

29. Name the longest key on the keyboard.

(A) Shift key
(B) Caps lock key
(C) Spacebar key
(D) None of these

30. Fill in the blank.

__________ is a type of computer that can be carried from one place to another.

(A) Desktop Computer
(B) Laptop
(C) Mobile Phone
(D) None of these

ACHIEVERS SECTION

31. Arrange the given steps to shut down a computer.
    (i) Switch off the UPS.
    (ii) Switch off the main power button.
    (iii) Click on Shut Down.
    (iv) Press the power button on Monitor.
    (v) Click on Start Button.
    (A) v, iii, iv, i, ii (B) iii, i, v, iv, ii
    (C) iv, v, i, ii, iii (D) i, iv, iii, ii, v

32. Salil wants to perform the following tasks:
    Play games
    Search information
    Listen to music and recorded sounds.
    Which of the following devices he can use?
    (A)  (B) 
    (C)  (D) All of these

33. Identify the following.
    It controls overall working of the computer.
    It is considered as the brain of the computer.
    (A) Monitor (B) Keyboard
    (C) Speakers (D) CPU

34. Which of the following statements is/are incorrect about the given part of computer?

(A) It has alphabet keys, number keys.
(B) It is used to type letters in a computer.
(C) It is called heart of the computer.
(D) It is an input device.

35. Match the following.

Column I		Column II	
A.	To create a copy of items onto a sheet of paper.	(i)	Used to fill the picture with colour.
B.	Caps Lock Key	(ii)	Clicking
C.	Color Tool	(iii)	Toggle key
D.	Pressing and releasing a button on Mouse	(iv)	Printer

(A) A-(iii), B-(i), C-(iv), D-(ii)
(B) A-(iv), B-(iii), C-(i), D-(ii)
(C) A-(i), B-(iv), C-(iii), D-(ii)
(D) A-(iv), B-(i), C-(ii), D-(iii)

INTERNATIONAL ENGLISH OLYMPIAD (IEO)

Mock Test Paper 1

I E O

INTERNATIONAL ENGLISH OLYMPIAD

Total Questions : 35 Time : 1 Hour

PATTERN AND MARKING SCHEME				
Section	**(1) Word and Structure Knowledge**	**(2) Reading**	**(3) Spoken and Written Expression**	**(4)Achievers**
No. of Questions		30		5
Marks per Questions		1		2

SYLLABUS

Jumbled Letters, Words : Their Meanings and Opposites, Identify the Word from the Picture, Making a Word, Feminine and Masculine, One and Many, Word Pairs, Odd One Out, Animals : Their Babies, Sounds and Groups, Nouns, Pronouns, Verbs, Articles, Prepositions, Adjectives, Basic Tenses, Punctuation, Comprehension (Prose and Poetry), Spoken and Written Expression.

Achievers Section: Higher Order Thinking Questions – Syllabus as per the above given syllabus.

WORD AND STRUCTURE KNOWLEDGE

1. Choose the correct word to describe the picture.

(A) Drawing room
(B) Bed room
(C) Kitchen
(D) Dining room

2. Identify the body part indicated with arrow.

(A) Nose (B) Hair
(C) Ear (D) Eyes

3. Unscramble the following letters to find a meaningful word

FEAL

(A) FLEA (B) LEAF
(C) ALFE (D) ELAF

4. What is the correct meaning of the word 'Command'.
(A) Control (B) Strike
(C) Order (D) Push

5. What is the correct meaning of the word 'Path'.
(A) Stairs (B) Way
(C) Footpath (D) River

6. Find out the opposite word for 'Loud'.
(A) Noise (B) Silent
(C) Tidy (D) Full

7. Find out the suitable opposite word for 'Inactive'.
(A) Sleepy (B) Hurry
(C) Noisy (D) Active

8. Identify the opposite gender for 'Bridegroom'.
(A) Groom (B) Girl
(C) Bride (D) Boy

9. Choose the correct word which is singular for 'Teeth".
(A) Tooth (B) Gum
(C) Jaw (D) Teether

10. Choose an appropriate word which completes the pair 'North and __'
(A) North East (B) South
(C) South North (D) South East

11. Find the odd one out.
(A) Summers (B) Sunny
(C) Rain (D) Winters

12. What is the young one of butterfl called as?
(A) Calf (B) Caterpillar
(C) Insect (D) Kite

13. Fill in the blank with appropriate countable noun.
There are ___ wheels in a car.
(A) Four (B) Three
(C) Two (D) One

14. Choose the correct pronoun for the following sentence.
Amay is playing hockey. __ likes playing hockey.
(A) He (B) She
(C) I (D) They

15. Choose the correct verb to fill in the blank.
The stars ___ at night.
(A) Burns (B) Glow
(C) Shine (D) Twinkle

16. Choose the proper article for the following sentence.
As a good human being, we should not tell ___ lie.
(A) A (B) An
(C) The (D) No article

17. Fill in the blank with the correct preposition according to the image.

There is a car and tree ____ of the house.
(A) Under (B) Near
(C) In front of (D) Beside

18. Fill in the blank with appropriate adjective.
India is a ___ country.
(A) Beautiful (B) Great
(C) Silent (D) Cute

19. Fill in the blank with the suitable helping verb.

It ___ raining yesterday.

(A) Will (B) Shall
(C) Did (D) Was

20. Hurray __ now we can play our favourite outdoor game.

(A) Hyphen (-)
(B) Question mark (?)
(C) Exclamatory mark (!)
(D) Full stop (.)

READING

Observe the image carefully for questions 21 to 23 and choose the correct option according to the question asked.

21. Sammer is ___ of Preetam.

(A) Behind (B) In front of
(C) Between (D) Around

22. Anushka is _____.

(A) Smiling (B) Crying
(C) Weeping (D) Sleeping

23. Four kids are _____ a rope.

(A) Pushing (B) Throwing
(C) Dumping (D) Pulling

For questions 24 and 25 read the following poetry and answer the questions asked.

"The sky is blue and sunny. Do you like the sunny sky?

The sky is black and rainy. Do you like the rainy sky?

The temperature is cold, it is winter. Do you like the winter cold?

The temperature is hot, it is summer. Do you like the summer hot?

I like them all!"

24. How is the temperature in winters?

(A) Cold (B) Hot
(C) Sunny (D) Rainy

25. What is the colour of rainy sky?

(A) Blue (B) White
(C) Black (D) Yellow

SPOKEN AND WRITTEN EXPRESSIONS

Select the correct option to complete the conversation for the questions 26 to 28.

26. Teacher: Do you know about Mrs. Pratibha Patil?

Anushka: _______

(A) Yes, she was the first female prime minister of our country
(B) Yes, she was the first female president of our country.
(C) Yes, she was the first defence minister of our country.
(D) Yes, she was the first pilot of our country.

27. Reshma: _____.

Aryan: Bye! Take care of yourself.

(A) Good night

(B) Nice to see you

(C) How are you?

(D) See you again! Bye!

28. Ishan: Does your brother know French?

Eesha: ___.

(A) No, he does not.

(B) My brother knows English

(C) No, he did not

(D) She can do.

Choose the correctly punctuated sentence for each sentence from 29 to 30.

29. What is the time by your watch

(A) What! is the time by your watch?

(B) What is the time; by your watch?

(C) What is the time by your watch?

(D) What is the time by your watch!

30. Lal Bahadur Shastri Atal Bihari Vajpayee I.K. Gujral were the prime ministers of India

(A) Lal Bahadur Shastri; Atal Bihari Vajpayee; I K Gujral were the prime ministers of India?

(B) Lal Bahadur Shastri, Atal Bihari Vajpayee and I K Gujral were the prime ministers of India.

(C) Lal Bahadur Shastri; Atal Bihari Vajpayee; I K Gujral were the prime ministers of India!

(D) Lal Bahadur Shastri and Atal Bihari Vajpayee and I K Gujral were the prime ministers of India!

ACHIEVERS SECTION

31. Unscramble the following letters to find the opposite word of unknown

USMFOA

(A) USFOAM (B) MOSFUA

(C) SOFMAU (D) FAMOUS

32. Mark the correct word which is feminine gender of 'Milkman'.

(A) Milkwoman

(B) Milkmaid

(C) Maid woman

(D) Milklady

33. Choose the suitable word partner for the word pair 'Fun and ___'.

(A) Entertainment

(B) Waterpark

(C) Food

(D) Fun

34. A ___ is the group of donkeys. Donkey makes a sound of ____.

(A) Herd, Sing (B) Pod, Roar

(C) Drove, Bray (D) Pod, Hiss

35. Fill the appropriate noun and pronoun in the given sentence.

Our national river Ganga rises from the _____ and ___ flows in many states of India.

(A) Mountains, She

(B) Himalaya, She

(C) Himalaya, It

(D) Uttarakhand, It.

Mock Test Paper 2

Total Questions : 35 Time : 1 Hour

I E O

INTERNATIONAL ENGLISH OLYMPIAD

PATTERN AND MARKING SCHEME					
Section	**(1) Word and Structure Knowledge**	**(2) Reading**	**(3) Spoken and Written Expression**	**(4)Achievers**
No. of Questions		30		5
Marks per Questions		1		2

SYLLABUS

Jumbled Letters, Words : Their Meanings and Opposites, Identify the Word from the Picture, Making a Word, Feminine and Masculine, One and Many, Word Pairs, Odd One Out, Animals : Their Babies, Sounds and Groups, Nouns, Pronouns, Verbs, Articles, Prepositions, Adjectives, Basic Tenses, Punctuation, Comprehension (Prose and Poetry), Spoken and Written Expression.

Achievers Section: Higher Order Thinking Questions – Syllabus as per the above given syllabus.

WORD AND STRUCTURE KNOWLEDGE

1. Identify the suitable punctuation for the following sentence.

   What is the time by your watch __

   (A) Hyphen (-)
   (B) Question mark (?)
   (C) Exclamatory mark (!)
   (D) Full stop (.)

2. Fill in the blank with suitable helping verb.

   She ___ go to school tomorrow.

   (A) Shall (B) Did
   (C) Will (D) Does

3. Read the sentence carefully and identify the adjective.

   Pandit Ravishankar was a very graceful sitar player.

   (A) Pandit Ravishankar
   (B) Very
   (C) Player
   (D) Graceful

4. Identify the preposition error in the following sentence and choose the correct preposition from the options.

   Rasika will be going in Mumbai tomorrow.

   (A) At in the place of in
   (B) On in the place of in
   (C) To in the place of in
   (D) No preposition is wrong

5. Choose the correct article to fill in the blank.

   Father wrote __ email to the principal of school.

   (A) A (B) An
   (C) The (D) No article

6. Choose the correct word to complete the sentence.

   The farmer ___ his fields

   (A) Ploughs (B) Digs
   (C) Burns (D) Waters

7. Choose the suitable pronoun word for the following.

   __ is a beautiful and colourful painting.

   (A) These (B) Those
   (C) That (D) There

8. Identify the noun from the given sentence.

   'That dress is very colourful'.

   (A) Dress (B) Very
   (C) Colour (D) Colourful

9. Identify the sound of wolf.

   (A) Roar (B) Bark
   (C) Howl (D) Hiss

10. Find the odd one out.

    (A) River (B) Island
    (C) Lake (D) Ocean

11. Choose an appropriate word which completes the pair 'Even and __'

    (A) Out (B) In
    (C) Odd (D) Equal

12. Choose the correct word which is plural of 'Leaf'.

    (A) Leafs (B) Leaves
    (C) Life (D) Leafes

13. Identify the opposite gender of 'lady'.

    (A) Leader (B) Gentleman
    (C) Owner (D) Boy

14. Find out the opposite word of 'Incorrect'.

    (A) Wrong (B) Right
    (C) Left (D) Correct

15. Find the opposite word of 'Polite.

    (A) Sweet (B) Rude
    (C) Bitter (D) Worse

16. What is the correct meaning of the word 'Collect'.

    (A) Hide (B) Finish
    (C) Provide (D) Gather

17. What is the correct meaning of the word 'Dark'.

    (A) Black (B) Brown
    (C) Light (D) Night

18. Unscramble the following letters to make a meaningful word.

    ERAHT

    (A) TREAH (B) REHAT
    (C) EARTH (D) HREAT

19. What are the names of two body parts enclosed in the circle?

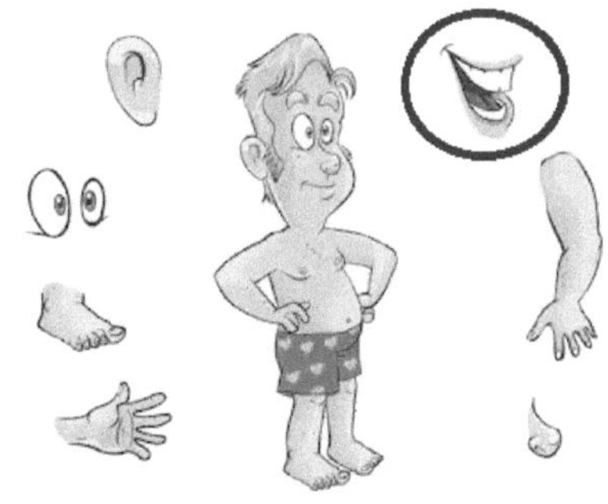

(A) Nose and tongue
(B) Teeth and nose
(C) Teeth and tongue
(D) None of these

20. Choose the correct word to describe the picture.

(A) Classroom (B) Playroom
(C) Bedroom (D) Drawing room

READING

For the questions 21 to 23 read the passage carefully and answer the questions.

We should follow the traffic rules. We should use the left lane for driving. There are three lights on the traffic signal with three different indications. When it is red light on the traffic signal it indicates that we should stop. When it is yellow light on the signal, it says that we should get ready to move. When it is green light at the signal it says that we can move now. To cross the road, we should use the zebra crossing when the signal is red for vehicles. Along the road we should use the footpath to walk.

21. Which lane we should use for driving?
(A) Right lane (B) Left lane
(C) Middle lane (D) Any lane

22. What does the red light signal?
(A) To stop (B) To run
(C) To move (D) To get ready

23. For walking along the road, we should use ______.
(A) Divider
(B) Middle lane
(C) Footpath
(D) Left lane of vehicles

Observe the image carefully for questions 24 to 25 and choose the correct option according to the question asked.

24. Four friends are playing an ____ game.

(A) Indoor (B) Outdoor
(C) Playground (D) Board

25. Manik is ___.
(A) Batsman (B) Bowler
(C) Referee (D) Goalkeeper

SPOKEN AND WRITTEN EXPRESSIONS

Choose the correctly punctuated sentence for each sentence from 26 to 28.

26. Wow what a wonderful day
    (A) Wow what a wonderful day?
    (B) Wow! What a wonderful day.
    (C) Wow; what a wonderful day?
    (D) Wow what a wonderful day!

27. Alas we lost the match
    (A) Alas! We lost the match.
    (B) Alas; we lost the match!
    (C) Alas; we lost the match?
    (D) Alas we lost the match.

28. Do you enjoy playing
    (A) Do; you enjoy playing
    (B) Do you? Enjoy playing?
    (C) Do! You enjoy playing?
    (D) Do you enjoy playing?

Select the correct option to complete the conversation for the questions 29 to 30

29. Junaid: Hello, how are you doing?
    Shahid: _____.
    (A) Hi, I am doing fine. Thank you!
    (B) Hello, how are you?
    (C) Hi, greetings.
    (D) I am fine, good bye

30. Mother: You should wake up early in the morning.
    Good boy: _____
    (A) No, I shall sleep more
    (B) Yes, I should play in the morning.
    (C) No, I should eat in the morning.
    (D) Yes, I shall wake up early from tomorrow.

ACHIEVERS SECTION

31. Fill in the blanks with helping verb and verb.
    Your best friend __ your favourite person in the class because he ___ with you.
    (A) Was, fight (B) Is, plays
    (C) Is, fight (D) Was, annoy

32. ___ Taj Mahal is situated in Agra. Choose the appropriate article to complete the sentence.
    (A) A (B) An
    (C) The (D) No article

33. Put the suitable preposition in the blank to complete the sentence.
    The travellers are waiting for the train __ the platform.
    (A) at (B) on
    (C) under (D) over

34. Choose the appropriate adverb to complete the sentence.
    Yesterday, we could not play our favourite outdoor game because it was raining ____.
    (A) Seriously (B) Extremely
    (C) Heavily (D) Boldly

35. Place the appropriate punctuations to enhance the clarity of the sentence.
    Do you want to eat Rasika
    (A) Do, you want to eat, Rasika?
    (B) Do you want to eat Rasika?
    (C) Do you want to eat, Rasika?
    (D) Do you; want to eat; Rasika?

Hints and Solutions

INTERNATIONAL MATHEMATICS OLYMPIAD (IMO)

MOCK TEST PAPER – 1

ANSWERS									
1. (C)	2. (B)	3. (B)	4. (A)	5. (B)	6. (C)	7. (C)	8. (C)	9. (D)	10. (B)
11. (A)	12. (C)	13. (B)	14. (C)	15. (A)	16. (C)	17. (B)	18. (B)	19. (B)	20. (C)
21. (A)	22. (A)	23. (C)	24. (D)	25. (D)	26. (D)	27. (C)	28. (B)	29. (A)	30. (C)
31. (C)	32. (A)	33. (D)	34. (C)	35. (B)					

1. (C) Cabbage is a vegetable while others are fruits.

2. (B) Table pairs up with chair.

5. (B) The figure has four sides, so it is a rectangle.

9. (D) From left hand (C) is third joker.

10. (B) The pattern followed here is that the object increases by 1 for every step.

11. (A) 6 more than 8 is, 6 + 8 is equal to 14

12. (C) The largest 4-digit number is 9999.

13. (B) Sum of all numbers on given cards is 8 + 3 + 9 + 7 + 4 is equal to 31

14. (C) 69 – 20 = 49

16. (C) The shape of an egg is oval.

17. (B) No. of books sold on Wednesday is 8.

18. (B) She has to pay ₹ 40 + ₹ 100 = ₹ 140

22. (A) Number of candles is 5 + 5 = 10

24.(D) Number of buses manufactured in the month of July and August altogether is 9 + 9 = 18

25. (D) The missing number is 9.

27. (C) Money she will get back is ₹ 40 – ₹ 25 = ₹ 15

28. (B) Length of the pencil is equal to nine clips.

29. (A) No. of keys that are in good condition are 13 – 4 = 9

31. (C) The jar with least capacity is the one with 40 units, as other three have 50 units, 60 units and 80 units.

32. (A) No. of working days is 4 + 4 + 5 + 4 + 5 = 22 days

33. (D) No. of circles in the given figure is 15.

34. (C) More money she requires is ₹ 55 – ₹ 40 = ₹ 15

MOCK TEST PAPER – 2

ANSWERS									
1. (B)	2. (B)	3. (C)	4. (A)	5. (B)	6. (D)	7. (B)	8. (A)	9. (B)	10. (B)
11. (B)	12. (C)	13. (C)	14. (A)	15. (B)	16. (B)	17. (B)	18. (C)	19. (C)	20. (C)
21. (B)	22. (C)	23. (D)	24. (A)	25. (A)	26. (B)	27. (C)	28. (C)	29. (C)	30. (D)
31. (B)	32 (D)	33. (B)	34. (B)	35. (A)					

2. (B) The number of fishes inside the net is 6.
3. (C) The shape is made up of 4 sides while others have 5 sides.
4. (A) Q is the longest pencil.
7. (B) Rectangle and circle alternate, Rectangle changes from horizontal to vertical to horizontal.
8. (A) The shape of a notebook is rect-angle.
9. (B) Teddy C is at the fourth position from the last.
10. (B) All are outlines of flag
12. (C) No. of chocolates left with her is 24 – 5 = 19
14. (A) The most ideal time is shown by the option (A) clock.
15. (B) He can buy the rocking horse since ₹ 100 – ₹ 45 = ₹ 55
18. (C) The sum represented by abacus = 45 + 23 = 68
19. (C) 93 – 4 = 89
20. (C) The number name of smallest two-digit number is Ten.
22. (C) *Ladoos* in the bowl are 47 + 25 = 72
23. (D) The name of the shape is cube.
24. (A) The money she has to take out from her piggy bank is ₹ 8.
26. (B) The number of shells Balu collected is 12.
28. (C) Latika's height is 168 + 12 = 180 cm
29. (C) No. of ice-creams left with him is 5 – 2 = 3
31. (B) Elephant is the heaviest.
32. (D) December has 31 days.
33. (B) No. of balls in the given figure is 48.
34. (B) Ball looks like a sphere.
35. (A) He has to pay ₹ 12 + ₹ 6 + ₹ 5 = ₹ 23

NATIONAL SCIENCE OLYMPIAD (NSO)

MOCK TEST PAPER – 1

ANSWERS									
1. (A)	2. (B)	3. (B)	4. (D)	5. (C)	6. (C)	7. (D)	8. (A)	9. (A)	10. (B)
11. (D)	12. (B)	13. (C)	14. (C)	15. (A)	16. (B)	17. (C)	18. (B)	19. (D)	20. (D)
21. (B)	22. (C)	23. (D)	24. (A)	25. (C)	26. (D)	27. (B)	28. (D)	29. (C)	30. (D)
31. (A)	32. (A)	33. (A)	34. (A)	35. (B)					

1. (A) R is a pink coloured shirt, rest are yellow in colour.
3. (B) Total 16 tigers are given. 4 groups of 4 tigers can be formed.
4. (D) As spoons are used to eat something from bowl, straws are used to drink water from water bottle.
5. (C) The small circle is moving clockwise in images.
6. (C) Mouse eats, breaths and moves. So it is a living thing.
7. (D) Carrots are the root part of the plant.
8. (A) Elephants are vegetarians i.e. they feed only on plants.
9. (A) Smell of the cake will help you to recognize it and nose is the sensory organ to detect the smell.
10. (B) Brushing teeth helps to keep the teeth clean and to prevent tooth decay.
13. (C) Natural things may be living (plants, animals) and non- living (rocks, mountains) both.
14. (C) Mustard is used for extraction of oil.
15. (A) Frogs can dwell on both land and water because they are amphibians.
16. (B) Skin in the sensory organ that helps to identify the feeling of touch.
20. (D) The inflated balloon shows that air provides shape to an object and absorbs space. Since originally the balloon was flat but later it became round. It shows that air exerts pressure since when more air was filled, then the balloon bursts.
21. (B) During winters days are small and nights are long.
22. (C) The symbol refers to the forecast of rain, so you should carry raincoat or umbrella for your safety.
24. (A) A band-aid, antiseptic and scissors are required for first aid purpose so they should be kept in a first aid kit.

25. (C) Helmet is for cycling and tube is for swimming. So both of these are correct pair.

26. (D) To stay fit you should eat more of fruits and vegetables and less of junk food.

28. (D) Ostrich is a two-legged and beak bearing bird and kangaroos have two legs but no beak.

29. (C) Among the given animals only monkey live on the trees and only elephant has a long trunk. All three of them eat plants.

30. (D) The stems of rose bear some thorns. So her finger got pricked with the thorn.

31. (A) Cow is a living thing, wooden table is made up of wood. Woods are obtained from the tree and trees are living things. Steel utensils are man made and non living things.

32. (A) Coconut provides all i.e. medicine, fibre, and oil

34. (A) Water is found present in air in a small amount.

MOCK TEST PAPER – 2

ANSWERS									
1. (B)	2. (A)	3. (D)	4. (C)	5. (C)	6. (D)	7. (C)	8. (A)	9. (D)	10. (C)
11. (B)	12. (A)	13. (B)	14. (A)	15. (D)	16. (C)	17. (C)	18. (B)	19. (D)	20. (A)
21. (D)	22. (D)	23. (B)	24. (A)	25. (A)	26. (A)	27. (C)	28. (B)	29. (D)	30. (A)
31. (C)	32. (C)	33. (C)	34. (A)	35. (C)					

1. (B) T is first, S is second and R is third from the right end.

2. (A) There are six flowers, so with two flowers in a group, total three groups could be formed.

3. (D) There are 2 circles and 8 triangles. So, the difference is $8 - 2 = 6$

4. (C) December is the last month of the year and new year starts from January. The sequence is November, December, January.

5. (C) Since the sequence is 50, 60, 70 the difference in the numbers is 10, the next number should be 80.

6. (D) It is very hot in June, so it is summer month. It rains in July so it is rainy month.

7. (C) 26th January is celebrated as Republic Day, those days are cold days (Not hot days).

8. (A) The shape of a full moon is like a big white ball when seen from Earth at night.

9. (D) A house is covered from all the sides with walls, doors and windows. So it protects us from sun, heat, rainfall and cold and strong winds.

10. (C) We cannot see air, we can only feel it.

11. (B) Football is filled with air, which occupies space and gives it a shape, so it is round in shape.

12. (A) The sign board indicates no parking zone.

13. (B) During prayer standing in the queue shows that you are disciplined and makes you a good kid.

14. (A) Zebra crossings (White and black strips marked on road) are made for pedestrians i.e. people walking on road. So, for crossing the road safely we should use zebra crossing.

16. (C) Rainy days are not cold days during which we wear woollen clothes. We use raincoat in rains.

17. (C) Milk has calcium which helps to make bones and teeth strong.

18. (B) The cartoon character is using earphones, so ears are in action.

19. (D) Eyes to see and fingers (skin) to touch.

20.(A) While writing a poem we hold a pen/pencil with our hands.

21. (D) Frogs make croaking sound.

23. (B) Calf is the baby of a cow.

26. (A) Soil provides water and nutrition for plants to grow.

27. (C) The image is showing the growth of the baby.

28. (B) A cycle cannot grow and breathe, so it is a non-living thing.

30. (A) Non-living things never grow.

31. (C) For burning a candle or anything, presence of air is necessary.

32. (C) The flowers grow into fruits when on tree. If flowers are plucked off, then they do not grow into fruits. So, if flowers are plucked, then number of fruits will reduce.

34. (A) The blown up ball is heavier than blown out ball because air has some weight.

NATIONAL CYBER OLYMPIAD (NCO)

MOCK TEST PAPER – 1

ANSWERS									
1. (C)	2. (B)	3. (A)	4. (B)	5. (C)	6. (D)	7. (A)	8. (C)	9. (C)	10. (A)
11. (B)	12. (C)	13. (B)	14. (A)	15. (A)	16. (B)	17. (B)	18. (C)	19. (C)	20. (C)
21. (C)	22. (A)	23. (A)	24. (C)	25. (B)	26. (A)	27. (B)	28. (D)	29. (C)	30. (D)
31. (A)	32. (C)	33. (D)	34. (D)	35. (B)					

1. (C) All of them are worn over feet except gloves.
2. (B) There are 2 groups of paper clips.
3. (A) 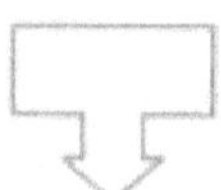
4. (B) Number = 21. There is gap of three between each number.
5. (C) 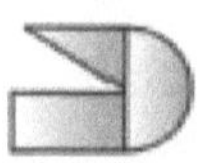
6. (D)  Computer is used to play games. Blender (A) is used to mix, Iron (B) is used to press cloth and Washing machine (C) is used to wash clothes.
7. (A) Monitor
8. (C) Keyboard
9. (C) Mouse. Two buttons, left and right are used to perform various functions.
10. (A) MS- Paint
11. (B) Smartphones
12. (C) Central Processing unit
13. (B) It is not the brain of the computer. CPU is the brain of the computer.
14. (A)  This is Google map used for finding locations.
15. (A) Smart watch is used to wear on wrist.
16. (B) Desktop
17. (B) Eraser Tool
18. (C) It is used for free-hand drawing.
19. (C)  - This is used for making straight lines not for filling colours in picture.
20. (C) computer, electricity, fast.
21. (C) MONITOR
22. (A)  Option B is for capitalizing the letters. Option C is used to delete letters by selecting or by moving forward and option C is used to delete letters by moving backwards.

23. (A) Ribbon Area

24. (C) Enter key

25. (B) 

26. (A) In banks, computers are used to maintain customer records and accounts.

27. (B) Mouse Pad

28. (D) Alphabet Keys

29. (C) 

30. (D) Monitor is an output device that is it shows information while other three are input device that is they help in giving information to the computer.

31. (A) Scrolling – Moving the mouse wheel up or down.
Enter key – Return key
Move the cursor down - 
Brain of a computer - CPU

32. (C) Left button Scroll
Wheel Right
Button Tail

33. (D) Schools

34. (D) It looks like a TV screen that displays information whatever we give as input.

35. (B) 2, 1, 4, 3

MOCK TEST PAPER – 2

ANSWERS									
1. (A)	2. (C)	3. (D)	4. (A)	5. (B)	6. (C)	7. (B)	8. (B)	9. (D)	10. (B)
11. (D)	12. (B)	13. (B)	14. (B)	15. (B)	16. (D)	17. (C)	18. (C)	19. (C)	20. (D)
21. (B)	22. (D)	23. (C)	24. (A)	25. (A)	26. (B)	27. (B)	28. (C)	29. (C)	30. (B)
31. (A)	32. (D)	33. (D)	34. (C)	35. (B)					

1. (A) 

2. (C) Number of squares = 8

3. (D) The 6th gift from the right end is E.

4. (A)  Car is most expensive.

5. (B) Gloves are worn in hand as cap is worn on the head. 

6. (C) CPU (Central Processing Unit)

7. (B) Printer

8. (B) The image is of a printer used for printing files.

9. (D) Arrow key

10. (B) Clicking

11. (D) Oval
12. (B) Spacebar key
13. (B) Wireless mouse
14. (B) Drawing Area
15. (B) To switch off the computer, first the start button on bottom left corner has to be pressed and then Shut down button has to be pressed.
16. (D) All of these
17. (C) It is used to draw circles -

18. (C) Line tool
19. (C) Double clicking
20. (D) 
21. (B) Used for pointing and selecting items on screen.
22. (D) ARROW
23. (C) Icons
24. (A) Scrolling. This action is done by moving the scroll button, it is used to move up and down.
25. (A) Smart watch
26. (B) 
27. (B) Candy Crush
28. (C) UPS (Uninterrupted Power Supply)
29. (C) Spacebar Key. It is used to give spaces between letters and numbers.
30. (B) Laptop
31. (A) 5, 3, 4, 1, 2
32. (D) All of these
33. (D) CPU (Central Processing Unit)
34. (C) It is called heart of the computer. Heart of the computer is CPU.
35. (B) To create a copy of items onto a sheet of paper – Printer
Caps lock key – Toggle key
Color tool – Used to fill the picture with colour.
Pressing and releasing a button on mouse – Clicking

INTERNATIONAL ENGLISH OLYMPIAD (IEO)

MOCK TEST PAPER – 1

ANSWERS									
1. (A)	2. (C)	3. (B)	4. (C)	5. (B)	6. (B)	7. (D)	8. (C)	9. (A)	10. (B)
11. (B)	12. (B)	13. (A)	14. (A)	15. (D)	16. (A)	17. (C)	18. (B)	19. (D)	20. (C)
21. (B)	22. (A)	23. (D)	24. (A)	25. (C)	26. (B)	27. (D)	28. (A)	29. (C)	30. (B)
31. (D)	32. (B)	33. (A)	34. (C)	35. (C)					

1. (A) This image has sofa, curtain, TV etc. which is generally part of drawing room.
2. (C) Ear helps in hearing.
3. (B) Leaf is part of a plant.
8. (C) He is the person (Male) who is getting married. Bride is the female version.
11. (B) All are seasons except sunny.
14. (A) Pronouns are used in the place of noun. In the given sentence Amay is a male so 'He' is the proper pronoun for him.
16. (A) Before the word starting with a consonant we use 'a' as the article.
35. (C) Himalaya is a noun because it is the name of a mountain. 'It' is a pronoun which is used in the place of Ganga.

MOCK TEST PAPER – 2

ANSWERS									
1. (B)	2. (C)	3. (D)	4. (C)	5. (B)	6. (A)	7. (C)	8. (A)	9. (C)	10. (B)
11. (C)	12. (B)	13. (B)	14. (D)	15. (B)	16. (D)	17. (A)	18. (C)	19. (C)	20. (A)
21. (B)	22. (A)	23. (C)	24. (B)	25. (D)	26. (B)	27. (A)	28. (D)	29. (A)	30. (D)
31. (B)	32. (C)	33. (A)	34. (C)	35. (C)					

1. (B) A punctation explains about the mood of the sentence. Here a question is being asked so question mark (?) should be used.
3. (D) An adjective describes the noun.
5. (B) Before the words starting with a vowel (a, e, o, u and i), we use 'an' as the article.
7. (C) Pronoun is a word which is used in the place of a noun.
8. (A) Noun is the name of a person, place or thing. Dress is the thing in the given sentence.
10. (B) All are water bodies except island.
20. (A) Students are sitting with books on desk. So, this is a classroom in school.
24. (B) They are playing football which is an outdoor game.
25. (D) Manik is standing in front of the goal post to save goals, so he is the goal keeper.
32. (C) Article 'the' is used for the specific definite noun. There is only one Taj Mahal in the whole world, so article 'the' would be used before it.
33. (A) Preposition 'at' is used to indicate a place.
34. (C) Heavily adverb specifies the type of rain.
35. (C) In this sentence someone is asking Rasika to eat.

9 789357 942263

Printed by Libri Plureos GmbH in Hamburg,
Germany